Rails to Disaster:
More British Steam Train Accidents 1906–1957

Rails to Disaster:

More British Steam Train Accidents 1906–1957

Malcolm Gerard and J. A. B. Hamilton

BOOK CLUB ASSOCIATES   LONDON

First published in 1984

Picture Research by Mike Esau

British Library Cataloguing in Publication Data

Gerard, Malcolm
  Rails to disaster.
1. Railroads – Great Britain – Accidents –
History – 20th century
I. Title   II. Hamilton, J. A. B.
363.1'22'0941   HE1783.G7
ISBN 0–04–385103–7

Set in 10 on 12 point Bembo by Nene Phototypesetters Ltd
and printed in Great Britain
by Biddles Ltd, Guildford, Surrey

Contents

Illustrations

Preface

Trains to Nowhere, a previous title in the 'Steam Past' series, was essentially a shortened version of the late J. A. B. Hamilton's much respected work, *British Railway Accidents of the Twentieth Century*, first published in 1967. Four accidents involving steam trains were not included in the revision: Elliot Junction, Ditton Junction, Darlington and Welwyn (1935). The chapters that dealt with these form the basis of this book and are largely as he wrote them, though with some updating as regards the present state of the sites. However, especially in the cases of the first and last of the four, I have taken the opportunity to deal briefly with other related incidents. I have also added track diagrams for Ditton and Darlington.

The rest of the book is my own original contribution to the subject. Within the parameters of the subtitle, I have chosen a range of railway accidents in most of which the human element is of special interest. Disaster tends to reveal man at his most heroic and his most fallible. Fate is, of course, very much involved in all accidents, but it really does seem to have worked overtime on some of them. Together with its acolyte coincidence, it seems to intervene capriciously in many cases – playing terrifying games with men and machines.

I have based my accounts largely on the official records of the inquiries that have followed all major railway accidents in Britain for well over a century. I am indebted, therefore, to the splendid work of the Inspectors who produced these reports. Serving officers from the Royal Engineers, they all seem to have brought an admirable combination of technical expertise and compassionate humanity to their task. J. W. Pringle and A. H. L. Mount, whose names figure repeatedly in these pages, inspire especial admiration.

After reading through other published material on some of these events, most of it dealing more briefly with the accidents, I have been surprised by the number of factual errors I have found. This includes, I regret to say, what is widely regarded as the definitive book on the subject and is undoubtedly an excellent and comprehensive survey of railway safety. Bear this in mind if you notice any discrepancies between my versions and those presented elsewhere – although I do not pretend to be infallible myself!

A word of thanks to all those who have assisted me in this work: the many employees of British Rail; Tyne and Wear Transport and their site contractors; Michael O'Donoghue and others at the British Library; P. W. B. Semmens at the National Railway Museum in York; Michael Leahy, who researched the Elliot Junction site updating; and most of all Mike Esau, whose contribution has extended far beyond his credited role of picture editor. I am most grateful to them all.

MALCOLM GERARD
May 1983

I
Elliot Junction
(North British and Caledonian Railways)

The first few years of the twentieth century were not amongst the happiest in the history of British railways, and 1906 was the worst of all. There were three serious accidents that year: the curve derailments at Salisbury and Grantham, which were dealt with in detail in *Trains to Nowhere*, and just before the year was exhausted there was a third major calamity. Twenty-seven years to the day after the Tay Bridge disaster, and less than 20 miles away, a Caledonian train was in collision with one belonging to the North British Railway at Elliot Junction – a mile or so south of Arbroath in Angus.

The Dundee to Arbroath line had been absorbed into the Caledonian, but as the North British began to push northward it was vested in joint ownership and formed part of the latter's east coast main line. The trains were staffed by the owning companies, but otherwise it was operated as a separate concern. The two controlling railways were not on good terms with each other and neither seemed much concerned to ensure their mutual venture was well run. In consequence it was not a well-managed line.

Elliot Junction was the diverging point of the long-closed Carmyllie branch. The station was no more than a single island platform and in those days was far from any significant habitation. The shelterless links of Arbroath Golf Club provided no protection from the winds howling in from the North Sea. It would be hard to find a bleaker spot in winter.

The winter of 1906–7 was similar to that of 1981–2; it set in early and by the last week in December nearly the whole of northern Europe was icebound. There were ten degrees of frost in north-east Scotland, accompanied by snow and gales. To quote *The Scotsman*: 'Wires hung in the air from the posts like cables of ice of the thickness of one's wrist, anon poles were uprooted and crashed to the ground before the biting blast.'

In these conditions, on Friday 28 December 1906, the 7.35 am left Edinburgh Waverley for Aberdeen. It was hauled by 4–4–0 no. 324 of the 317 class – Holmes' last design. The train was in the charge of Driver Gourlay, one of the senior drivers from the Haymarket depot in Edinburgh. He had twice driven Royalty – one of the occasions being a special for the Kaiser. In view of the prevailing weather the train did well to reach Arbroath only an hour late at 10.41. Part of the delay was caused by a mishap earlier

WHERE TWENTY-ONE PEOPLE LOST THEIR LIVES: THE DERAILED EXPRESS ENGINE AND THE WRECK OF THE LOCAL TRAIN AT ELLIOT STATION, NEAR ARBROATH.

1. Elliot Junction. Looking north on the following day with clearance work in progress. No. 324 still lies where it toppled over, and in the foreground can be seen the twisted chassis of the last coach of the Caledonian train into which it ran.

Illustrated London News

that morning to a southbound goods train which broke into three parts at Downie siding – a mile south of Elliot Junction. When this was discovered at Easthaven, 2 miles further south, the driver conceived the notion of returning to the junction so that he could get behind the broken portions and then propel them on to Easthaven. Not unnaturally, in the heavy snow, the wagons were promptly derailed and this had caused single-line working between Easthaven and Elliot Junction.

All the telegraph lines were down and no one had thought to send a message to Arbroath, so the single-line working was not known about there until the afternoon. The pilotman, Inspector Souter, was not provided with an engine to carry him back and forth so he had to cover the 3 miles on foot at times.

Once the Aberdeen-bound express reached Arbroath it came to a full stop. Both lines northwards – the North British to Montrose and the Caledonian to Forfar – were blocked. There were said to be six trains stuck in the snow. For over four hours the express hung about

14

Arbroath station in the hope that it could eventually be sent on. By three in the afternoon it was still snowing hard and the passengers were getting restless. They saw no prospect of reaching their destinations and began to importune the stationmaster to send the train back to Edinburgh. Finally he agreed to do so. Meanwhile a Caledonian local, which had come up earlier from Dundee, was sent off from the down platform at 3.10 with about fifty passengers.

No. 324 was still on its train facing north. It ought to have been turned for the return journey, for a long tender-first run, especially in such weather, was undesirable for every reason. But the turntable was awkwardly placed at St Vigean's Junction, ½ mile or more to the north, and it was said that the points were blocked, or that there were coaches on the down line. The shed foreman at St Vigean's maintained that the engine could have been turned, and, as was pointed out at the inquiry, if the down line was blocked the engine could have been sent along the up line. Driver Gourlay, when he got back to Edinburgh that night and was interviewed by the press, maintained that the turntable was too small to take his engine, which was certainly not the case. In any event he never asked to have it turned; he knew it would be no good, he said. It looks as if the decision to return was made at short notice, and nobody really bothered about which way the engine was to travel. Tender-first running was so common on the Joint Line (the Caledonian train had come up that way) that even in these conditions it did not seem out of place.

So Gourlay and his passengers set out on their return journey, as an all-stations train this time. Since the block telegraph system was out of action the time interval system had been introduced, and the Caledonian train was given a sixteen-minute start. At Arbroath South, Signalman James Beattie came down from his box and told Gourlay to 'take care of himself' – a common phrase, it was explained, to use for warning drivers to go slowly and with due caution. Both Gourlay and the front guard Kinnear had already been warned to the same effect by the stationmaster. The single-line working beyond Elliot Junction was still not known at Arbroath.

The first ¼ mile or so out of Arbroath is in cutting, which offered comparative shelter. From it the train emerged to face the full fury of the storm. The plight of the enginemen, with snow driving into the cab, coal dust being whipped up by the wind and lumps of coal blown on to the footplate, can be imagined. As for Guard Kinnear, his window immediately became blocked by snow, and any lookout was impossible.

Meanwhile the Caledonian train had been held up at Elliot Junction, waiting for Souter to foot it back from Easthaven. Carnegie, the stationmaster, at length decided that it would be safer to have the train drawn forward, while the passengers would be warmer in the waiting room. He had just decided to get them out when no. 324 appeared out of the storm travelling at about 30 mph and crashed into the rear of the waiting train. The latter's last three coaches were wrecked, as was the front coach of the North British train. No. 324 mounted the debris and fell over on her side, her driving wheels revolving furiously for ten minutes until Ogilvie, the Caledonian driver, crawled into the cab and shut the regulator. He also extricated Gourlay, who was buried in coal but not badly injured. The fireman, however, though he was rescued after seven hours, died.

Besides the fireman, twenty-one passengers were killed. Among them was an MP, Mr A. W. Black, Member for Banffshire, who died in hospital.

It was in character that the Joint Line should have no proper breakdown equipment, and lifting operations had to wait until Messrs Shanks' Foundry in Arbroath could send some 8-ton jacks to the scene. The breakdown train did not arrive until the early hours of the following morning.

The injured passengers were taken into the waiting room. As a sidelight on travelling conditions before train-heating became general, we read that the uninjured passengers placed rugs, wraps and other articles at the disposal of the casualties.

Quite clearly Gourlay was at fault. He maintained that the Elliot Junction home signal had given him a false clear, but after the accident it was found to be drooping only ten degrees under the weight of the snow on the wire. Gourlay had to agree too that if, working under the caution system, the signal was at clear, it would mean that something had gone wrong. With better reason he claimed that there should have been a fogman out at the Elliot Junction

distant. But in any event his speed in those conditions was reckless. It transpired that while waiting at Arbroath a passenger had taken him into the Victoria Bar, situated right by the station and open, in those days of more liberal licensing laws, throughout the day. His behaviour after the accident had seemed 'peculiar' and he was later arrested and charged with 'Culpably and recklessly driving his train while under the influence of drink'. He spent several days in the cells at Dundee before being released on £300 bail.

Under recently passed legislation, despite there being a charge outstanding, a public inquiry was held. In Arbroath Sheriff Court, in front of a jury, the evidence was heard and two questions engrossed the participants: was the driver drunk and ought there to have been a fogman at the distant signal?

With regard to the first the evidence was conflicting. A parcels clerk, who had gone onto the footplate about 2.30, testified to seeing Gourlay leaning out of the cab window as if he were

Illustrated London News

2. Elliot Junction. Here seen from the front, the stricken locomotive lies amid the bleak snowscape of this isolated location.

3. Elliot Junction. The rear of a southbound HST glides past the foundations of the old island platform as it is today. On the right is the track leading onto the truncated remnant of the former Carmyllie branch.

M. D. Leahy

vomiting. He added that the driver's speech was thick. A doctor and a police sergeant who saw Gourlay after the collision affirmed that he appeared to be drunk but other witnesses declared with equal emphasis that he appeared shocked but certainly *not* drunk. Gourlay himself said that he had had just one small whisky with a passenger in the Victoria Bar and had then come straight out after refusing a double. He also claimed to have refused a flask of something offered to him by a passenger whilst he was on the footplate.

The fogman question resolved itself into a contest between the North British Railway, as Gourlay's employer, and the Joint Line – which was responsible for the signalling. The latter's lawyer questioned the NBR's traffic inspector: 'Do you think it reasonable,' he asked, 'to have kept a fogman at that signal with no trains from 9 am to 3.30 pm?' 'I know he would have been kept on the North British line,' came the reply; 'I have never known a greater need for fog signalling in all my experience.' He had nothing to do with the Joint Line, he was at pains to explain, but he had heard that it hardly ever used fog signals. Gourlay had had them at Easthaven going down, but that appeared to be the exceptional case. It was stated that since the accident fog signals had been introduced – sufficient admission of the previous negligence.

Predictably, the jury found that Gourlay was at fault in not obeying his instructions to go carefully. Nothing was said about his being drunk. The jury also found that fog signals should have been used and that the North British train should have been held up longer.

The evidence at the inquiry, and the jury's findings, had evidently made the police think again about the charge of drunkenness, and when Gourlay came to stand his trial the indictment

17

had been altered. It now read that: 'He failed to proceed cautiously, failed to bring his engine to a stand at Elliot Junction signal box . . . and so caused his train and engine to collide and killed the twenty-two named persons.' He was found guilty by a majority verdict of ten to five and sentenced to five months' imprisonment, but the sentence was remitted.

The Board of Trade's Inspector, Major Pringle, in his report on the accident, brushed aside Gourlay's story of the single 'nip'. He held that: 'The lack of intelligence, or of caution and alertness, displayed by Driver Gourlay were, in part at all events, induced by drink, the effects of which may possibly have been accentuated after he left Arbroath by exposure to the weather.' He went on to say that he thought the proximity of the Victoria Bar was not a very desirable feature of the station surroundings and it would be better for the staff there if a coffee shop and refreshment room was substituted. The reaction of the staff is not recorded! In any event the pub still flourishes there.

Major Pringle roundly condemned the goods driver for attempting to propel wagons through the snow – that was sheer folly and bound to lead to derailment. In fact, he had a lot of unflattering things to say about the operation of the Joint Line; he was especially critical of the failure to see that Arbroath was informed of the single-line working that had been introduced. If it had been, Gourlay would have had some warning that the Caledonian train might be held up.

Now, more than three-quarters of a century later, the up and down tracks of the main line from Dundee to Aberdeen still separate to accommodate the island platform of Elliot Junction – even though the platform is no more. When the passenger service to Carmyllie was withdrawn in 1929, the station's *raison d'être* had gone, but the southward development of Arbroath sustained it for more than another

generation until the final train called in 1967. The footbridge, that had long since replaced the one at the time of the accident, has lost the central flight that led to the platform but is still in use to give access across the tracks to the beach and the playing fields that are laid out now at the end of the links between the railway and the sea.

There is still the stunted vestige of the branch line, but it runs only a few hundred yards into a wood and exists only to provide a shunt-back into the siding of the Metal Box Company in the Arbroath Industrial Estate that today dominates the location. A simple four-lever lineside frame is all that is needed now for what remains of the junction, being worked, as are the level crossing gates where the branch crosses the A92, by those staffing the infrequent traffic.

The desolate site of 1906 has essentially gone, but in 1982 it was still possible to find at least one person who remembered it as it was on that dark December day. He was actually there, living in the same nearby cottage, at the time of the accident. Though only eight years old then, it understandably made an indelible impression on his young mind and he recalled how they had torn sheets to make bandages and had given shelter and refreshment to some of those involved.

Despite the development of the area, it can still be a bleak scene on the seaward side when the snow sweeps over it in the depths of winter. Snow, of course, has always been the railwayman's greatest natural enemy and has been the cause of many a disaster over the years. The most notorious was at Abbots Ripton in 1876 when a passenger train ran into a goods, and another passenger train ran into the wreckage. Signals frozen in the clear position were the immediate cause of that horrific incident and amongst the several changes in operating procedure that ensued, probably the most important was the decision that in future signals would normally remain in the danger position until needed to pass a train through, instead of at clear most of the time.

Nowadays, with mostly colour light signals and so many track circuits – not to mention Automatic Train Control being in general use – the chance of collisions like those at Elliot Junction or Castlecary (another in snow, dealt with in *Trains to Nowhere*) are surely impossible. And yet in an isolated, snow-coated rural cutting in Buckinghamshire, on the old Great Western and Great Central Joint line, as recently as December 1981, it happened again. A young, newly qualified signalman in the Gerrards Cross box told the driver of a DMU to pass a signal at red and thus sent him on to crash into the back of an empty stock train that had stopped so its driver could try to clear a snow-laden bough over-hanging the line. The signal was locked at red because the first train had not cleared the section and the track circuit indicator showed this. But the signalman, with no experience of working in such extreme weather conditions, thought that the intense cold had affected both the instrument and the signal so he over-rode all the safety devices and assured the driver of the second train that it was safe to proceed. Four died in that incredible affair – including two children on their way to school and the driver he had waved through. It happened in the same kind of blizzard that had swept Elliot Junction all those years before, and it meant that Seer Green was added to the awesome list of places where trains have come to grief.

It would seem that even today there is no way to guard completely against that most enigmatic and unpredictable of factors: the human one.

2
Ditton Junction
(London and North Western Railway)

In the unlovely countryside of south Lanca-
shire, close to the town of Widnes, Ditton
Junction is situated on the former North
Western line from Crewe to Liverpool. It was
here on 17 September 1912 that a holiday express became derailed as it ran through a crossover and fire broke out as a result of escaping
gas.

It was the driver's ignorance of the unusual
layout of the junction that caused the accident.
At that time it was approached from the east by
three double lines. The centre line was from

Crewe, descending on an embankment at a
gradient of 1 in 114 from the Runcorn Bridge
over the Mersey. Flanking it on either side were
two different routes from Warrington; these
will be referred to as Warrington north and
south. Warrington north does not concern us,
except that its presence may have helped to con-
fuse the driver. From Ditton onwards there
were two double lines towards Liverpool,
Warrington south becoming the slow line and
the main line from Crewe continuing as the fast
track. The unusual feature of the junction was

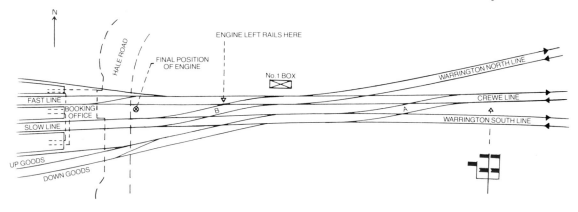

SIMPLIFIED DIAGRAM OF DITTON JUNCTION

20

the provision of two crossovers from the Crewe line to Warrington south within 100 yards of each other.

The first of these, which is marked as A on the diagram, was to enable freight trains from the Crewe line to reach a pair of goods lines which diverged from Warrington south at that point; the second crossover, B on the diagram, was close to the Hale Road overbridge just before the station, and was the fast-to-slow crossover as well as forming the means by which trains could pass from Warrington north onto the slow main line to Liverpool. Crossover A could also serve as a fast-to-slow crossover of course, but was not normally used as such. It was perfectly

4. Ditton Junction. The wall of wreckage which the carriages formed under the Hale Road overbridge has been cleared away, though fragments of the rolling stock can still be identified. The huge crane is ready to lift 'Cook' back onto the rails.

possible for a driver not well acquainted with the route to be unaware that there were, unusually, these two crossovers and thus to misread the signals that control them. The rules require that drivers are familiar with the roads they travel when in charge of a train, but on more than one occasion this rule has not been strictly observed. This is a classic example.

The signals in question consisted firstly of splitting distants: two signals side by side, one for the fast line and one for crossing over to the slow line via crossover B. There was no distant for crossover A. Secondly there was a gantry, shown in the diagram, with three home signals reading (right to left): main line, crossover to down slow via B and, slightly lower than the other two, crossover to down goods via A. The

first two carried distants under them for Ditton No. 2 box. The Warrington north tracks had no signals at this point. Three sets of tracks and three signals; it would be all too easy for a driver coming down the main line in the middle to read the centre signal as applying to him and indicating that he was continuing straight ahead. This is undoubtedly what happened in this case.

The 5.30 pm summer-only from Chester, with through coaches from Afon Wen, consisted of three six-wheelers and four eight-wheelers marshalled in that order. There were also, incongruously for a holiday express, two Great Western horseboxes next to the engine, a 2–4–0 Precedent class named 'Cook' which weighed (without its tender) less than 36 tons.

5. Ditton Junction. The crumpled front of the engine being manoeuvred back onto the track having been swung up into position from its original resting place. The tender is clearly visible in the background, still lying where it was flung. The substantially damaged brickwork of the bridge pier graphically identifies the point of impact.

It seems odd that the LNWR, which by this time was well provided with modern engines, should entrust a fast train to such an old stager. 'Cook's' leading wheels had no side-play, which gave the engine a rigid wheelbase of over 15 feet. A bogie engine would probably have kept the rails.

The key element in the accident, however, was the fact that the engine was entrusted to a driver poorly acquainted with the road, and to discover how this came about we must go to Llandudno Junction shed where he was based. His name was Robert Hughes and he was young for a driver in those days, being only forty-one. He was in fact a spare driver who had doubtless been called upon to help out with the summer traffic. By the same token his fireman on this trip was actually an engine cleaner, eligible to go firing as required. The 'Arranger of Engines', as he was called, at Llandudno Junction was a certain Owen Owens, who was only a driver

BBC Hulton Picture Library

himself – 'a man of no authority', as the Inspecting Officer put it.

Owens told the inquiry that Hughes had said to him: 'I'm all right for Liverpool', which he had taken to mean that Hughes knew the road. Unfortunately Hughes was not 'all right'. He had made the journey many times as a fireman it was true, and had signed the road book as a driver four years previously, but in those four years he had only driven to Liverpool on ten occasions and on none of these had he been put across from the fast to the slow line at Ditton. His experience of the line as a fireman was worth very little for the signals were on the left-hand side – the driver's side on the North Western – and he would not therefore have been called upon to look out for them. Hughes himself however had no misgivings. He could have called for a pilot at Chester, but did not do so.

So 'Cook' came hurtling down the gradient from Runcorn at a good 60 mph, Hughes evidently believing that he was set for the straight road. So he would have been in the normal way, but it happened that a London express was close behind him, which was due to pass his train before Liverpool was reached. So the unsuspecting driver found himself switched on to the crossover. 'Cook' left the rails, turned on its side, slithered along the track still steaming and fetched up against a pier of the overbridge, from which it dislodged a quantity of brickwork. As it struck the bridge the boiler sheared away from the firebox. The leading horsebox was thrown right over the bridge and landed on the station platform beyond. The second horsebox was cut in half and one half landed either side of the bridge. The horse in the first vehicle leapt out startled but unhurt; in the severed one the horse was, not surprisingly, killed – though the groom travelling in the same wagon escaped.

The three six-wheelers formed a compact mass of wreckage under the bridge and against the wall of the booking office; no passengers in the first two coaches survived. One eight-wheeler came to rest on top of the bridge; the remaining three kept upright though all were damaged.

The whole train was gas-lit and, although fire did not break out immediately, within a few minutes it began to show in the wreckage. There was a plentiful supply of water, as well as of skilled fire-fighters from the chemical works nearby, but gas-fed fires are not easily extinguished. This one blazed for a couple of hours and the whole of the front part of the train was consumed. Driver Hughes had died instantly; his fireman was rescued after many hours but died in hospital. Thirteen passengers also died, but, although unrecognisable after the fire, it was established that mercifully none had been burned to death.

The poignancy of the aftermath is movingly captured in the words of a newspaper reporter at the time, and they give too the right period flavour. He wrote: 'The charred luggage lay in heaps, together with hats, caps, fur boas, luncheon baskets, fruit, sweets and holiday literature.' He went on to mention that the rescue work was hampered by the crowds of spectators; the selfishness of the ghoulish is no new phenomenon.

At the inquiry the Inspecting Officer, Lt-Col Yorke, criticised the signalling installation. It was unnecessary and confusing, he said, to have a distant signal for one crossover and not for the other. A single distant, which would stand at caution when a train was to be crossed, was all that was required. If the fast-to-slow line distant were retained, it should carry on its post a speed restriction warning sign. As regards the driver's knowledge of the road, the Chief Mechanical Engineer maintained that Hughes was thoroughly conversant with it. The Inspec-

6. Ditton Junction. Its wheels all back on the metals, but with its firebox and cab torn away in the crash, what remains of 'Cook' stands forlornly waiting to be towed away.

BBC Hulton Picture Library

tor did not agree; Hughes should have applied for a pilot at Chester, he said.

If a latter-day Hughes was to come along now, he would be presented with quite a different picture. Ditton Junction is now part of British Rail's London Midland electrification, and three colour light signals away he would have the first warning of the divergence in the form of a double yellow. The second light would show a single yellow and the third a red. Just before he was brought to a stop, the signal would change to yellow and show the 'feathers' – a diagonal row of white lights indicating that he was to be crossed over. Furthermore at each light a hooter would sound in the cab and the brakes would be automatically applied if necessary. There is only the one crossover between the tracks now, and that is aligned at a much more gentle angle so that even 'Cook' might hope to negotiate it safely at speed.

Ditton is in many ways an excellent example of the seventy years of railway progress that separate the present from that late summer day in the calm before the first of the cataclysmic world wars. The brick Hale Road bridge which 'Cook' struck has been replaced by one of reinforced concrete. A new push-button signal box now surveys the scene from a site opposite that of the old No. 1 box. The Warrington north line has gone as has some of the incidental trackwork, but a large new sleeper works with creosoting equipment has been built in fields to the west of the station, being reached by track extending from where the Runcorn local trains used to stand.

The station itself, now known simply as Ditton, is served only by a handful of rush-hour trains on weekdays. Demoted to the last stage short of closure, the rest of the Liverpool–Crewe local service ignores it and the Inter-City electrics which bustle through have never acknowledged its existence at all.

3
St Bedes
(North Eastern Railway)

The year 1915 was a black one for the railways. As a vital part of the war effort they were under a lot of strain. There is, of course, nothing like pressure for discovering weaknesses that might survive less stressful conditions, and that no doubt played a part in making it such a misadventurous twelve months.

Disaster began with the year itself, for the very first day had only just finished dawning when ten people died in a crash at Ilford on the Great Eastern. An express from Clacton ran into an up suburban train on points at the London end of the station as the latter was joining the main line. The engine, no. 1813, hit the seventh coach of the local and was thrown off the track. The coach behind it was badly damaged as were several on the other train. New Year's Day was not then a holiday in England, and both trains were crowded with a normal Friday morning complement so the casualty toll was correspondingly high. A full 500 sustained some degree of injury. The cause was as simple as it was classic: the engine crew had missed a distant signal at danger. It led the Inspector at the inquiry to urge some sort of automatic train control at such signals. It was not the first such recommendation by any means, but the GWR was still alone in recognising the value and need of such equipment, which it had started developing in 1906. The GER merely had detonators at some of their home signals.

In the summer another ten died at Weedon (of which event we shall hear more in Chapter 12), but both Ilford and Weedon pale into insignificance on either side of the accident that took place on 22 May near the Cumbrian border with Scotland, for this was the year of Quintinshill – the worst-ever disaster on a British railway. That horrendous happening, dealt with in *Trains to Nowhere*, overshadowed the rest of a period that would have been bad enough in any case. People died in no fewer than eight train crashes in 1915; Kinsale, Smithy Bridge, Pollockshaws, and Newark being also added to the inventory of inquests.

The catastrophic year dragged on until Christmas was at last in sight to lend some badly needed cheer. Then, incredibly it seemed, there was another disaster on the Quintinshill pattern – though mercifully not on the Quintinshill scale. It happened at St Bedes Junction on

17 December on the North Eastern Railway's line between Newcastle Upon Tyne and South Shields. Nineteen died and eighty-one were injured, ⋅compared with more than 200 killed and many more than that hurt at Quintinshill. By normal railway standards, however, it was still a major disaster.

St Bedes Junction was the point on the line, between Jarrow and Tyne Dock stations, where a twin-tracked goods line branched off to Tyne Dock Bottom. The signal box was on the up (Newcastle-bound) side directly opposite the junction itself. The site is at the bottom of gradients ranging from 1 in 100 to 1 in 660 for 1½ miles in each direction on the main line. It is, however, at the top of a steep gradient – as steep as 1 in 49 at one point – from the aptly named Tyne Dock Bottom on the branch. This climb often necessitated a banking engine assisting the more heavily loaded freight trains leaving the dock, and on 17 December such an engine was in use for the 6.50 am departure.

It was still dark at that time and, in contrast to the bright, clear morning seven months earlier at Quintinshill, it was foggy. Driver William Hunter was on the footplate of the banking

engine, a six-coupled tank locomotive, no. 2182, with his fireman Robert Jewitt. Bob Jewitt was only eighteen and had started with the North Eastern three and a half years previously as an engine cleaner. He had graduated to temporary fireman status and had been acting continuously for seven months as fireman with Driver Hunter on no. 2182. The engine came up, chimney-first, behind the guard's van of the 6.50 which was composed also of twenty-one loaded and ten empty vehicles.

The guard's van had the regulation two red side lights and red tail light, but the banking engine had a red light on the front and a green one on the bunker end. This strange arrangement was not at all unusual on this branch since it saved the bother of changing the lights round after the five-minute run up to St Bedes! There being no passenger trains on the line up from the dock, it was not felt necessary to couple assisting locomotives to the trains they were pushing. The signals approaching the junction were clear, so the train was able to proceed unhindered through the crossing, over onto the up line and on towards Jarrow. No. 2182 was still at the tail as the end of the train passed the signal box, but

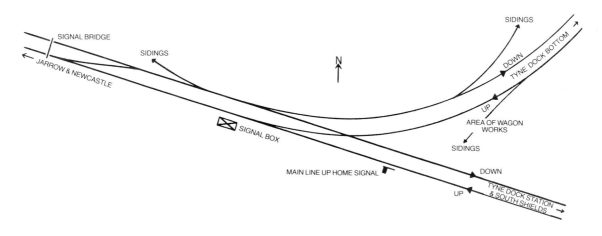

SIMPLIFIED TRACK LAYOUT AT ST BEDES

with its job done it dropped back from the departing train and came to a stand at its usual place: about 90 yards beyond the box just past a signal bridge that spanned the line. The bridge carried a number of down-line signals, including the one in which the crew of the now light engine were interested. This would allow them to reverse back through a crossover close to their rear, onto the down line and thence back onto their branch. Driver Hunter sounded the whistle to let the signalman know that they were clear of the points and they waited for them to be changed and for their signal to be lowered.

However, it was the signal for a down goods train making for the branch that cleared first. This meant that they would be waiting there for at least another couple of minutes so Hunter told young Jewitt to change the green light on the back to a red one.

The down goods went by and, having given it time to clear, Hunter blew the whistle again. Still the points did not move and their signal remained firmly at danger whilst once more another one went down instead. By this time Hunter was beginning to get a little anxious. He told his young fireman that he would have to send him to the box in accordance with Rule 55. Jewitt couldn't remember the rule – by its number anyway – so his driver explained it to him. At least he explained his interpretation of it, which may not have been quite the same thing. Rule 55 tended on some lines to be acknowledged more in the breach than the observance. It required, essentially, that if a driver was detained at a signal not covered by special regulations, and it did not clear when the whistle was sounded, then the fireman (or guard if there was one and he was nearer) must go to the signal box and ensure that the signalman was aware of the train's presence. Within three minutes in clear weather, said the rule, but

immediately if it was foggy. For obvious reasons it could be a very tiresome rule to follow and therefore many drivers tended to stretch the time before they felt obliged to comply with the regulation. Hunter, who apparently saw the instruction as simply intended to remind a signalman that he was being kept waiting unnecessarily, had reasoned that, since another down signal was off, the points could not be changed and his signal cleared until a train had passed. It was futile then, as he saw it, to send his fireman trudging back to the box while this situation existed.

Driver Hunter and Fireman Jewitt had started working together at almost exactly the time of the Quintinshill fiasco, where the proper application of Rule 55 could have averted the tragedy. Hunter had been a driver for less than two years but had been on or around engines for twenty-three years and, even if he had not given much thought to that particular rule before, what had transpired on that day in May such a short time ago should have made him reluctant to bend it now. Perhaps what happened on the Caledonian Railway was not considered to be relevant to the 'superior' North Eastern. Jewitt, young and comparatively inexperienced though he was, must have heard of the rule even before Hunter's explanation, and again it seems odd that the story of the nation's most disastrous railway accident had seemingly not impressed itself on him – at least in so far as a fireman's duties were concerned. We should not, of course, underestimate the courage it would have taken for an acting fireman to question or prompt his superior on a footplate. At eighteen he is perhaps to be forgiven for leaving all the initiative to the much older man in charge.

Whether Jewitt set off for the signal box just before, during or after the next down train passed is not certain, but he was nearly there when the metals alongside him began to vibrate

Illustrated London News

7. St Bedes. In the left-hand picture no. 1867 of the South Shields–Newcastle train is seen at the foot of the up-side embankment where it came to rest. Beside it is part of the wreck of the light engine, no. 2182, thrown there after being struck by the third engine involved. In the right-hand picture is the partially burnt out second coach of the up passenger train, a third-class vehicle, no. 1571, being lifted during the difficult and depressing aftermath of the accident.

with the approach of an up train – a train on the same line as the engine he had so recently left. He rushed on and attracted the attention of the signalman who opened the window and asked him what was the matter.

Signalman William Hodgson had worked in St Bedes box for forty years, nearly the whole of his working life. He had been on duty for only about an hour on that cold winter morning when the up goods had come off the branch at 6.55 am. The use of assisting engines from Tyne Dock Bottom, although it had been going on for some time and was obviously necessary, had never been officially endorsed by the Company, and therefore no bell code for it had been added to the list authorised there. It was left to the man in the St Bedes box to notice when a banking engine was bringing up the rear of a train. More often than not there was one with that particular train, but on this foggy morning, close to the

shortest day of the year and so still dark, he did not see one. He told the subsequent inquiry that he was sure that the final light on the train was red. He knew a pilot engine might be showing a red or a green light to the rear but added later that, since he had seen *three* red lights, he was convinced that the brake van was the end of the whole train. Despite the fog he could see the back lights of the signals on the bridge 92 yards up the line – the signal bridge where the light engines waited to reverse – but he could not see the rails at all. It was not untypical of conditions at that spot at that time of the year in the early mornings, and did not merit calling out fogmen or going over to fog working. It would seem, however, that it was dense enough to have an unusually deadening effect on sound that day, for he also said that he did not hear any of the engine's whistles. Certainly there is no doubt that he was unaware of the light engine until Fireman Jewitt came rushing up, shouting and waving his lamp.

Hodgson, on hearing Jewitt's news, told him to turn his lamp to red and put it up against the oncoming train. He then dashed over to the levers and threw the signals to danger in a desperate attempt to stop the up passenger train he had happily accepted from Harton box five minutes before – having had clearance from Jarrow in respect of the goods.

It was too late. The home signal went to danger just as the engine was passing it. The 7.5 am South Shields–Newcastle passenger service was headed by 0–4–4 tank engine, no. 1867, running chimney-first. Driver William Smith never saw the signal return as the loco swept past it at 30 mph. Nor did his fireman, Frank McArdle, who was breaking coal at the time. Smith saw no hand-lamp being waved below him in the gloom and noticed nothing unusual when passing the box, Hodgson not having had time to start waving a lamp himself. A moment later Smith saw the back of Hunter's engine looming up only a few yards ahead. He turned off the steam and went to apply the brake but there was no time. After that, all he remembered was that the engine began to oscillate and then came to an abrupt stop before moving a little again a moment or two later. His fireman was not even aware that they had left the rails, let alone hit another engine. He heard a noise and the locomotive began to shake and then came to a stop. He got out and was amazed to find himself on the embankment.

Driver Hunter, on the light engine, had heard the rumble heralding the up train and, although not yet convinced that the unthinkable was about to happen, he decided to get his engine moving forward just in case. When he applied steam, however, the engine was priming and he had only just got going when he saw the approaching headlights closing fast from behind. He blew the whistle frantically but to no avail. With his engine making only about 5 mph, and the other making over 30, the now inevitable collision occurred. He felt his engine leave the rails and then he was knocked unconscious, coming round to find himself standing in a field at the bottom of the twenty-foot embankment some little while later.

The light engine had been derailed fouling the down line. The second engine had run off to the left and descended the embankment with its chimney end near the bottom of the slope and the bunker near the top. The leading vehicle, a brake-third, had uncoupled and run past its engine and lay with its underframe against the bunker. The second carriage, an ordinary third, was telescoped into the back of it and had completely smashed all three of its passenger compartments. The rear bogie of the second vehicle was still on the rails as was the rest of the train, undamaged.

Up the line a little way, quite unaware of the drama being enacted, Driver George William Taylor was on a 2–4–2 tank engine, no. 671, running bunker-first with an empty stock train from Hebburn to South Shields. Approaching St Bedes he saw the distant signal at danger, Hodgson not having had clearance from Harton box, so he shut off steam and started gentle braking. He had brought his speed down from 30 mph to around 10 mph and was fully prepared to stop at the home signal if necessary. He was peering through the fog, which had become more intense as he neared the bottom of the gradient, to see the position of the home, when suddenly he saw a flash of fire and steam and knew nothing more until he came to on the down-side embankment. He was not even injured, nor was his fireman, and in this respect they were luckier than those on the other two footplates at the time of the first collision. Drivers Smith and Hunter and Fireman McArdle were all three injured but were, in their turn, lucky to be alive considering the circumstances.

Taylor's engine had hit the derailed light engine, throwing it over onto the up-side embankment where it struck the locomotive already there and came to rest facing the direction from which it had been coming. The down train's engine in striking it had itself been deflected onto the embankment on its own side. Its leading coach was derailed but remained upright and finished up overlapping its counterpart from the other train, burning with it in the ensuing conflagration.

The eighteen passengers who died were mostly in that other front carriage and were probably killed by the immediate effects of the collision itself, but the fire quickly destroyed the wooden coachwork and consumed the bodies entirely. This made identification difficult and autopsies impossible. In the second carriage, however, not all those who perished were dead when the fire broke out. Their terrible plight was witnessed by those who could not reach them in time.

For some idea of what it was like to be in one of those front carriages when the collision occurred, we turn to the splendidly-named Samson Tolliday, who emerged as the drama's principal hero. Tolliday had been a driver on the North Eastern for thirty-seven years but was not on duty at the time and was travelling as a passenger. He had joined the train at Tyne Dock station and, unable to see an empty seat in the three compartments of the front brake-third, he had got into the second-to-front one of the following coach. He described the collision to the inquiry thus:

> The first I knew of there being anything wrong with my train was a very severe jerk . . . There were two jerks with a short interval in between, and during that interval my vehicle seemed to continue on. After the second jerk the carriage seemed to be going to pieces; the sides and bottom of the carriage seemed to be going in altogether. I think there were about four other passengers in my compartment. They seemed to lose control of themselves and I told them to keep very cool.

> We tried to get the doors of our compartment open but we could not. Then I got the window down . . . I got out of the window [and] told the other passengers to do the same and keep themselves very cool. All the passengers got out of my compartment.

Samson Tolliday was obviously an ideal man to have around in such a situation. Amongst his many attributes, he was experienced in first aid. Having ensured that all necessary rescue services had been summoned, he got tools from the brake van and rescued three people from the compartment ahead of the one in which he had been travelling. He was working to free a fourth when he saw fire spring up from a gas cylinder close by, possibly ignited by hot ash from one of the pipes that were being smoked in the compartment at the time of the crash. He got an extinguisher but was unable to check the blaze which had by then got hold of the woodwork. He quickly finished releasing the fourth passenger but the heat was too great for him to do anything about the remaining two.

He got other extinguishers and tried to stop the fire spreading until his face was burnt and he was obviously losing the battle. Abandoning the futile fight, he went to help others who were trying to get people out of the first carriage before fire reached that too. His cool competence and initiative undoubtedly saved several lives and he was justly lauded for his efforts on that terrible morning.

Principal among the others who had helped in the rescue of passengers from the first coach were Driver William Rowe and Guard William Dunlop. (William seems to have been much favoured as a Christian name thereabouts – there are no less than five in this story.) Rowe and Dunlop were also commended for their part in the life-saving work. They had been in charge of the down goods – the first train to pass the light

8. St Bedes. The site of the accident as it looked in May 1982. The picture was taken from the up line by the foundations of the demolished signal box and shows Bede station under construction for the Tyne and Wear Metro. The new alignment to the branch line is seen on the far right-hand side.

Malcolm Gerard

engine whilst it was standing at the signal bridge. Their train had been stopped at the distant signal near the top of the branch, waiting for the Dock Bottom box to let them proceed. On learning of the crash they had run back to help and assisted in getting some of the trapped and injured out of the leading carriage. They then had the prudence to uncouple each of the last five undamaged vehicles and push them clear of the fire which would undoubtedly have spread to the third coach at any moment.

The inquiry was conducted by the same officer of the Royal Engineers who had investigated the Ilford collision that had started the year's deplorable railway chronicle. P. G. Von Donop, who was by now a Lieutenant-Colonel, was understandably very critical of the casual way that banking engines were operated on the Dock Bottom branch and suggested that the Company should introduce the bell code that notifies a signalman that an approaching train is assisted by a pilot engine at the rear. The correct and consistent use of head and tail lamps on such engines was also urged.

Signalman Hodgson was, of course, condemned for failing to notice the presence of this particular banking engine – especially as there was a more than 50 per cent chance that the goods train would have one to assist. However, after deliberating on all the evidence and testimony, he reserved his principal criticism for the driver. Once the engine had finished its job, and was standing light at the signal bridge, it was a full seventeen minutes before Hunter observed the rule he should have followed almost at once. This failure to comply with Rule 55 was the principal cause of the double disaster and Hunter bore a very great responsibility for the results.

The Inspector accepted that nothing could have been done to prevent the second collision once the first had occurred. The signals were already at danger and there was not time to warn the driver of the down train who was proceeding quite correctly. There was less than a minute between the two collisions – some thought only a few seconds. It was the time between the abrupt stop that Driver Smith had mentioned and the slight further movement a moment later. The second movement was the effect of the light engine being thrown against his after the down train had struck it. He was dazed, of course, and his perception of time possibly impaired, but Samson Tolliday defined the 'short interval' between the two jerks he experienced (each being one of the collisions) as only a moment. The fire that Driver Taylor had seen flash in front of him just before he hit the derailed light engine, was the locomotive's spilt fire and not the subsequently burning carriages.

As regards the aftermath of the collisions, the Inspector stressed, as he and his colleagues had so often had occasion to do before, the desirability of changing from gas to electricity as the means of lighting railway carriages. So many lives had been lost because of fires started or fed by gas in accidents like those at Hawes Junction, Ais Gill and the notorious Quintinshill only a few months before. The case for getting rid of gas as quickly as possible was now surely unarguable. At St Bedes, the evidence that the fire actually originated with gas was more conclusive than in any previous case and was an object lesson of the most decisive kind for the railway owners. For the previous three years the North Eastern had been installing electric light in all its new rolling stock but no steps had been taken to convert existing stock, and about 85 per cent of its carriages were still gas lit.

But for all the entreaties and the experience of St Bedes and the other funeral pyres, the blind intransigence, born of economic considerations, was to prevail generally for well over a decade more. So even as late as 1928 we can still find an accident in which gas caused a major fire. That was at Charfield (see *Trains to Nowhere*) and was yet another double collision, this time involving two goods trains and an LMS express. It was the final crash to be followed by a significant fire. It took a long time and a lot of lost lives to bring electricity to the last carriage, and one might feel that the recommendations of the Board of Trade Inspectors should have been backed up with some effective legislation. But that December morning on Tyneside was still in the first full year of the war and there were other priorities.

St Bedes has seen a lot of changes since 1915. In the 'twenties the line to South Shields was electrified using the third rail system. Some twenty or so years ago the whole of the Tyneside electrification was dismantled and DMUs introduced. Then, at the end of the 'seventies, the imaginative Metro system was begun and the Tyne and Wear Transport Executive began taking over suburban Newcastle lines from British Rail. In June 1981 the last BR passenger services were withdrawn from the South Shields line and once more work began to electrify it – though this time using overhead catenary.

St Bedes signal box has been demolished and the junction removed. The line towards Tyne Dock Bottom still exists, however, although its main function is to serve the Simonside Wagon Works at the upper end, but it is now reached by way of a new alignment of the former down main line. British Rail freight trains are thus kept separate from the new Metro services as the latter use only the old up line through Hebburn and Jarrow, with passing places at stations, until the new alignment begins just about where no.

2182 stood all that time at the signal bridge. The Metro takes over both tracks towards South Shields from this point eastwards.

Next to the foundations of the old box is the up platform of the location's most obvious new development, for a station – called simply 'Bede' – has been built to serve the three busy industrial estates that have grown up around the site. With its automated turnstiles and ticket machines, which mean that – like all the other stations on the system – it needs no supervision, it is the epitome of advanced urban transport design and thinking. In keeping with this up-to-date approach is the centralised control of signals and points and the use of radio to keep in constant touch with the drivers of the one-man-operated trains. It's a whole new kind of railway to the one that existed sixty-eight years before Bede station sold its first automatic ticket and the events of that dark December day earned the scene a less happy place in the annals of the area.

St Bedes saw human beings behaving with both weakness and strength. Had fate seen fit to reverse the roles of drivers Hunter and Tolliday that morning, then St Bedes would have been unlikely to figure in the gazetteer of railway tragedy. One cannot see Tolliday waiting such an extraordinarily long time at that signal before carrying out Rule 55. But then, as a casting director, fate has all too often favoured the tragic option, and in that respect nothing has changed.

4
Little Salkeld
(Midland Railway and London Midland
& Scottish Railway)

We visit now the Midland Company's spectacular line over the Pennines. Built as part of the Midland's main line from London to Scotland, this stretch of track has seen more than its share of railway dramas. The notorious accidents near Hawes Junction and Ais Gill in the second decade of the century, together with the one near Settle in 1960, were described in *Trains to Nowhere*. This time we travel further down the line to one of those places that disaster has visited more than once. Fifteen years and ½ mile separate the two accidents at Little Salkeld, a tiny rural parish between Lazonby and Langwathby about 18 miles south of Carlisle.

Following a twilight period as an unstaffed halt, the station at Little Salkeld finally closed in 1970 when the local stopping trains were withdrawn from the route, leaving Appleby as the only place in the timetable between Settle and Carlisle. Its neighbours still receive the odd visit from one of the occasional enterprising Dales Rail specials, but Little Salkeld does not even merit that slight recognition. The buildings stand forlorn: the waiting room serving as a

store and sometime workshop for permanent way maintenance. The signal box has gone and a colour light signal stands sentinel by its site. The points have all long since disappeared as have the sidings, though a firm still uses the old goods yard via the road access. It is, in fact, a perfect representative illustration of the decline of the rural wayside station, imbued with all the nostalgia for a lost way of life.

Things were very different back in 1918. The Great War still had ten months to rage, and the railways were weary from three years of war effort, when the 8.50 am 'Thames–Clyde Express' left St Pancras on its way to Glasgow on Saturday 19 January. All had gone routinely throughout the morning and the train pulled out of Leeds promptly at 1.45 pm. Driver Whitworth was making very good time and was actually a few minutes early at Ais Gill on the summit of the High Pennines line. With the regulator barely open, he let the speed build up to 55 mph down the long descent which was comfortably within the limit for the section. The engine was a class 4 compound 4–4–0, no. 1010, and the train consisted of an eight-

Illustrated London News

9. Little Salkeld, 1918. In the first of these two newspaper pictures no. 1010, with chimney apparently still smoking, leans against the side of the cutting where the drag of the ballast finally brought it to a stop. The wreckage of the brake van and leading coach has been cleared from the up line and is strewn along the lineside. In the foreground some of the van's contents can be seen among the debris being taken away. In the second picture the landslip in the up side of the cutting can be seen behind the tender of the locomotive attached to the rescue crane working at the back of the derailed train.

wheeled bogie van and ten assorted passenger carriages. No. 1010 was driven from the right-hand side and afforded Whitworth an uninterrupted view of the road ahead. The signals were all clear down through Appleby and on past Long Marton, New Biggin, Culgaith, Langwathby and Little Salkeld stations. At this point the line has reached the bottom of the 30-mile incline and begins an easy right-hand curve which goes along an embankment and into Long Meg cutting. Over the many years he had worked the line, Whitworth had got into the habit of taking special notice round this bend. There had been a distant signal, where the line straightened out in the cutting, which belonged to the Long Meg block section. The block post had been abandoned three years previously but old habits die hard – especially when there is no particular need to break them. It was now 3.57 pm and still clear daylight. Having observed the end of the curve ahead and, seeing nothing unusual, he did a routine check of the cab's instruments and glanced at the fire that his mate, Costello, was tending. When he looked out again a few seconds later he saw to his horror that a mass of sludge was covering the rails just in front of him. He had only time to throw over the brake handle as the engine ran into the obstruction. It mounted the sodden soil and was showered with mud and water as it dropped down onto the ballast and ran on for 180 yards until the drag brought it to a standstill leaning over towards the left. Whitworth turned and saw the van behind the tender shoot out and turn over on its side across the up line with the first coach riding up on top of it. The rest of the train followed the path taken by the engine and kept fairly upright. Only the last carriage remained on the rails.

Although both the vehicles that had taken the full effect of the derailment had gas lighting there was mercifully no fire – unlike the terrible conflagrations following the accidents up at Ais Gill and Hawes Junction a few years earlier. Seven passengers died however, as a result of the crash, and about fifty other people were injured – many quite seriously. The crew of the locomotive escaped with only a few bruises, though much shaken. The guard in the brake van behind them was much more badly bruised, and cut and wrenched as well, but he was even luckier to escape really serious injury in view of what had happened to his van. He was trapped by luggage which fell on top of him as the vehicle turned on its side and it was quite some time before he was released by some passengers.

Col J. W. Pringle was the Inspecting Officer at the inquiry, as he had been at the ones held after Ais Gill and Hawes Junction. This time his job was much easier and less painful. It had been an act of God that could not reasonably have been foreseen or prevented, and was an open and shut case with no human beings to shoulder the blame.

The man in charge of that stretch of line was a foreman-platelayer called Spreadbury. He had been doing his normal scheduled inspection of the line that afternoon and had passed the point of the landslip twice in the hour before the accident occurred – the last time only twenty-three minutes beforehand. There had been no sign of movement having taken place in the cutting and nothing to suggest that it might. The ground was very wet and the drains were full, but there was no water escaping from the face of the cutting nor spilling over its edge. He had walked about a mile up the line when he heard the express approaching and then the chilling sound of the crash.

The nature of the substance that lay over the line was described as that of 'fermenting balm' which, even several hours later, could only with difficulty be handled with a shovel. It must have resembled a wave of mud as it rolled down the

1 in 3 slope of the cutting. A few seconds was all it had taken – the few seconds that the driver's attention was away from the track ahead. Not that he could have slowed the train much in those few moments as the ooze had spread out thirty feet across the level, obliterating the rails and laying its trap for the speeding train.

The weather, that constant culprit in man's love-hate relationship with nature, was the real villain, of course. Three days previously, following heavy frost, there had been a three-inch fall of snow in the area. This had not lain long when a substantial and rapid rise in temperature had led to an unusually fast thaw. The snow had virtually gone by the afternoon of the fatal day and rain had been falling intermittently all morning with a particularly heavy downpour at about 2 pm. It was probable that the frost had affected the normal drainage through the soil and it was therefore unable to cope with the quickly melting snow. This had resulted in water collecting in exceptional amounts at the base of the depression just above the site of the slip, with the underlying clay preventing it escaping at anything like the rate at which it was accumulating. The whole area had become so waterlogged that the weight of the mass of liquid had burst its way through the side of the cutting.

Something comparable happened on another occasion further up the line at Dent Head, but fortunately a driver had noticed a bulge in the side of the cutting in time to give warning and prevent any traffic encountering the enormous

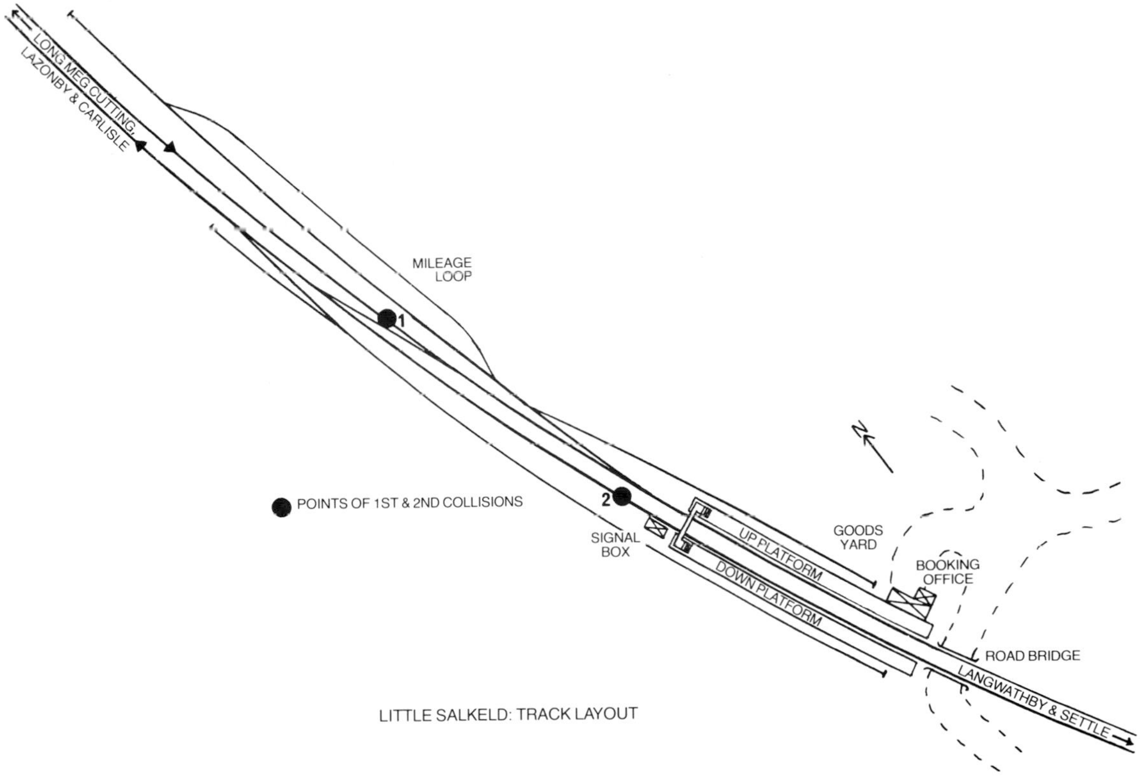

LONG MEG CUTTING.
LAZONBY & CARLISLE

MILEAGE
LOOP

1

POINTS OF 1ST & 2ND COLLISIONS

2

SIGNAL
BOX

UP PLATFORM

DOWN PLATFORM

GOODS
YARD

BOOKING
OFFICE

ROAD BRIDGE

LANGWATHBY & SETTLE

LITTLE SALKELD: TRACK LAYOUT

avalanche of earth that descended soon afterwards. The line was closed for weeks that time and single-line working was then introduced for the six months or so that it took to build a huge retaining wall to prevent a recurrence.

Cutting slips have always been a hazard of railway operating from the earliest days. One of the first serious train accidents was caused by a landslip at Sonning on Christmas Eve 1841. A 2–4–0 Leo class engine called 'Hecla' ran into a great mound of earth dislodged by exceptionally heavy rain. Eight passengers died in the two third-class open-sided coaches which were crushed by the following laden goods wagons that comprised the bulk of the train – such was the regard in which the railways held their poorer customers. The dangers of such slips led eventually to the installation of wires running along especially vulnerable cuttings which, if displaced or broken by earth movement, convey a warning to the signalmen on either side.

The Settle–Carlisle line is open to some of the bleakest of English weather as it traverses the inhospitable heights of the Pennine hills, running over bridges and viaducts and through tunnels and cuttings more numerous than virtually anywhere else in Britain. It has therefore always been particularly prone to the problem of landslips and closely watched by the permanent way men. The tell-tale signs of an impending slip have nearly always been spotted by the keen eyes of the men who tramp the tracks in all climatic conditions, and disasters have nearly always been averted. The Long Meg incident was the exception that proves the rule. Landslips figure again in the Friog chapter, which is another tale of two accidents at the same place. Those two were *both* cutting slips, but the second incident at Little Salkeld was something very different.

No. 1010 was little damaged by its upsetting experience and was soon back in service. Many times in the following fifteen years it passed the point at which it had happened. And so it did on 10 July in 1933. Painted now in LMS livery, no. 1010 was this time on the up line heading the London-bound 'Thames–Forth Express' due out of Carlisle at 12.44 pm. It was a dry, though sunless, summer Monday with no danger of landslides as it entered Long Meg cutting at about 1.09 pm.

Driver Slee was running well to time having made up the minute he had been late leaving Carlisle. Little Salkeld distant signal came into sight 1,000 yards ahead and it was 'off'. His speed was up to nearly 60 mph and his fireman, Brown, was shovelling on more coal ready for the long climb ahead. From this direction the curve at the north end of the station was a left-hand one and it was not easy to see the home signal from his position on the right of the footplate. Since the distant had been at clear there was no reason to suppose that the home might not be. He couldn't remember later whether or not he saw the home signal but it made little difference, for it would have been too late to avoid what happened next.

An 0–6–0 goods engine, no. 4091, was propelling three wagons as it reversed over a trailing crossover from the down to the up line at the north of the station – right into the path of the express. The inevitable violent meeting of the two trains occurred before any action could be taken by either driver to reduce the severity of the impact. The collision had an extraordinary effect. No. 1010 hit the near-side corner of one of the wagons and its right-hand motion assembly and low-pressure cylinder were torn off, as was the front buffer on that side with the buffer-beam being pushed back into the frame. Simultaneously the speeding engine came into contact with the still-moving tender of no. 4091, this being next to the wagon the compound had struck. Deflected from its path, no.

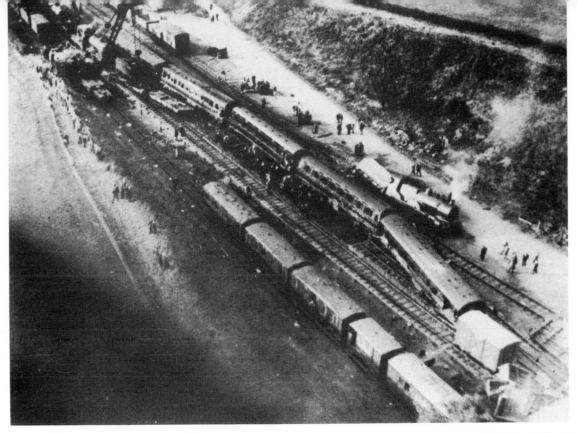

10. Little Salkeld, 1933. Fifteen years later no. 1010 once again found itself derailed and canted over to its left at Little Salkeld in one of history's oddest coincidences. In this aerial view, the damage at seat level of most of the coaches can be clearly seen – as can the more extensive damage to the leading brake-third. In front of that first carriage is an LNER 10-ton covered goods wagon (no. 724565) which was the fourth vehicle in the goods train, the front one of those left on the down line during the shunting. Behind it, in the bottom right-hand corner of the picture, are the shattered remains of the following wagon, an LMS 8-ton highside (no. 711814) which was completely broken up. The crane at the left-hand top corner is dealing with the tender of the goods engine.

1010 broke away from its train and ran off into the roadway beyond the adjacent siding, coming to rest some 20 feet to the left of the main line. It finished up, very badly mangled, leaning over at an angle of sixty degrees with its wheels buried and about 90 yards ahead of the point of collision. Slee was not badly hurt but Brown was more seriously injured and took many weeks to recover.

As it had hit the goods wagon, no. 1010 had thrown it clear of the line. With its fortuitous detachment from its train the compound had made it possible for the coaches to run on and lose speed more slowly and, although (except for the last one) all were derailed by their contact with the goods engine that was still fouling their path, they remained essentially in line and upright, and there was no telescoping. There were, of course, still two more wagons left out of the three being shunted, and these were pushed, partly derailed, in front of the coaches. The leading coach, actually an LNER six-wheeled yeast van, hit the wagons and propelled them along for about a hundred yards until they were totally

39

derailed, and it was itself deflected to the right and onto the down line where the freight train's remaining eight vehicles were standing. The wooden yeast van was demolished, and the following all-steel corridor brake-third coach was badly damaged in the process.

The goods engine had ripped the sides of all but the last of the six carriages that formed the rest of the train behind the yeast van. The stock had withstood the impact well and it was only this tearing, which was at seat level, that led to the list of casualties being as high as it was. Even so, none died. It was a lightly loaded train with no more than sixty aboard, and about half received some injuries, or suffered from shock, with three being kept in hospital.

Further up the line in 1960, over the hills near Settle, in the last significant British steam train accident of all, the coaches of another lightly loaded express suffered a similar fate when a derailed freight engine ripped their sides. There were fewer injured that time but five were killed. The only death at Little Salkeld in 1933 was that of the unfortunate driver of the shunting locomotive, whose name was Shaughnessy, and at sixty-four was on the point of retiring. He survived the crash only to die from his injuries the next day – poor reward for a lifetime of conscientious service, especially since he was in no way to blame for what had happened.

What indeed *had* happened? The results we have seen, but what of the cause? To understand this we must go, as is all too often the case, into the signal box overlooking the scene.

Little Salkeld box was at the northern end of the down platform, 120 yards south of the point of the initial collision and only 16 yards south of the second one involving the remainder of the freight train on the down line. It belonged to the growing number of signal boxes that were open for only part of the time that their sections were in use. On the Midland Division of the LMS alone there were at that time about 200 such boxes with part-time weekday working. That represented around 17 per cent of the total number. It was obviously essential that the Regulations were rigidly followed when opening and closing these cabins to ensure the safety of trains in section at such times. In view of the enormous number of occasions on which boxes throughout the country had gone through the switching in and out procedures, it was a testimony to the diligence of the operating staff that there had been only one accident (at Cleckheaton way back in 1905) in which the opening or closing of a signal box had been a significant factor. Only one, that is, until that summer's day in Cumberland in 1933.

Little Salkeld box was equipped with drophandle, three-position, three-wire, needle-pattern block instruments. There were no track circuits. Like its neighbouring boxes at Lazonby and Langwathby it had a small Midland-type frame, but unlike them it had no telephone. There was a phone in the booking office, but that was 90 yards away across the line on the up platform.

The principal function of the box was to control the shunting of freight trains. Sometimes this was to allow an express to overtake, sometimes to facilitate the dropping and collecting of wagons from the small goods yard on the up side, which had shed accommodation and a mileage loop. There was also a lie-by siding served by trailing points about 200 yards north of the box on the down side and, of course, the crucial trailing crossover between the running lines. There were distant, home and starting signals for both directions, and altogether eleven levers were in use out of the twelve provided. The box was open only as and when necessary to work any of the points, but otherwise the section was switched out and all the signals left in the clear position.

Since such part-time boxes obviously did not provide full-time work for signalmen, those employed at station boxes had to act as porters as well. Since the end of March of the year in question, the man employed here had been a Scot from Ayrshire called Hannah. He had had a curious history with the Company since first joining as a signal box lad at Irvine when he was fifteen. He was promoted to porter, left the Company, rejoined, was made redundant, rejoined again, trained as a signalman at West Kilbride and was made redundant a second time. He had rejoined for his fourth period of service as a temporary porter at Ardrossan in 1927 before going back to West Kilbride, and later Bar Hill, to continue his training as a signalman. He passed as porter-signalman in November 1928 and then went to Pinwherry as a signalman in October 1929. In this capacity he served also in Carlisle No. 9 box, Whithorn, and Castle Kennedy. Now, at thirty-three, he found himself in the somewhat inferior position of porter-signalman again at this wayside station over 100 miles away from his home at Kilwinning. He was probably not, therefore, best pleased with his lot.

On that July day he came on duty at 10.30 am and was due off at 8 pm. Just before noon he opened the box for the first time that week to let an up goods drop off a wagon and then wait whilst the up 'Thames–Clyde Express' overtook it. The express sped through at 12.24 and he sent the goods train off in its wake at 12.28, closing the box immediately afterwards. He then went to lunch.

His official mealtime was 1.30 to 2.30 but he was in the habit of taking it an hour earlier, as had been his predecessor. This was because there was a down freight due at about 1.30 and sometimes it required the box to be opened. This could make him late for his lunch and cause problems with his landlady. Since there was no passenger train due to stop, nor any other compelling reason for him to be there just then, 12.30 seemed a more sensible time for lunch and suited everyone. It had not, however, been officially agreed and his supervisor, the stationmaster at Langwathby, had not been told.

His lodgings were in a nearby railway cottage and he was surprised, and not a little annoyed, to hear the freight train approaching at about 1.05 pm – some twenty-five minutes ahead of time. There was nothing for the train to pick up but he was not given advance notice if any wagons were to be dropped off, so did not know if it would require the box to be opened on this trip. He hurried back to the station and got there as the train was pulling in. It stopped just before the crossover and the guard, Graham, unhooked between the third and fourth wagons and beckoned the driver on over the points.

'I've a wagon of coal for you,' Graham said to Hannah as the latter approached. 'It took the other man about fifteen minutes to put one wagon off,' replied Hannah testily as he recalled the train he had dealt with before lunch. He went up into the box and the guard heard him throwing the levers over. The signals went to danger and the points moved. Graham waved to Shaughnessy to bring his engine back through the crossover onto the up line from which the goods yard could be reached. There were three sets of points to go through before the wagon of coal (the third of the three wagons still attached to the engine) could be left. Directly he saw the guard waving, Shaughnessy gave steam and the locomotive moved backwards pushing the three trucks through the points. A couple of seconds later Graham saw no. 1010 bringing the express round the bend, but the wagons were already entering the up line and there was nothing he could do. If the other train had come into sight a few moments earlier all would have been well, for he would not then have given the hand signal. If . . . how often after disaster has that provoking little word been used?

Hannah was distraught, as well he might have been. He had assumed that the express had gone through whilst he was at lunch as it would have done if the freight train had arrived nearer its scheduled time. He ran out of the box in a highly distressed state, having sent 'Obstruction Danger' to the signalmen on either side. Graham got the keys of the booking office from him and phoned Langwathby.

It was some time before the hapless Hannah was sufficiently recovered to be interviewed, and, when he was, his account differed somewhat from that of the others involved. The essential facts were ferreted out by the investigating officer, Lt-Col Mount, and a sorry tale they made.

Hannah had almost totally disregarded the rules governing the opening of the box. The block switches were, as previously mentioned, of the three-position type, that is: 'Through', 'Intermediate' and 'Open'; the purpose of the 'Intermediate' position being principally to enable the operator to ascertain the position of the block and peg up accordingly before turning to 'Open'. Hannah claimed that he had never been told to use this intermediate position – a claim disputed by both his predecessor, who had explained the working of the box to him, and his supervising stationmaster. He also claimed that it was not the practice on the line when switching a box in to telephone the boxes on either side to find out what trains, if any, were in section. On this latter claim he was supported by the signalman at Langwathby, Strong, who said that, although he knew of the regulation, he had never done so himself – even

11. Little Salkeld, 1982. The appearance of both buildings and platforms belies the long time that has elapsed since this attractive little rural station was host to a passenger. The signal box stood at the end of the down platform in the right-hand foreground. The colour light signal is the only prominent added touch to a scene that is much as it must have looked that fatal lunchtime half a century ago when Hannah hurried back to deal with the goods train.

Malcolm Gerard

with a phone in the box – and no one had suggested that he was wrong not to do so. Signalman Lane at Lazonby was also in broad agreement on this point. The block instrument there had been installed for only a year but he had never considered it necessary to phone before using the switch. Lane, however, proved an unreliable witness and there were serious errors in his train register, so his opinion as to what was or was not 'necessary' was of dubious value.

There was, nonetheless, a feeling amongst many railwaymen that prior use of a telephone weakened the significance of the block and that reliance solely on the indicators was not only sufficient but positively desirable. Some Companies did not require the phone to be used in this way, and others only required it to identify the boxes being opened and not for obtaining train information. The fact remained that the LMS *did* require its use for information on trains in section and this regulation was being widely flouted.

Lt-Col Mount as usual got to the truth of the matter in the best detective tradition. Hannah had obviously been caught out by the early arrival of the down goods train while being improperly absent from his post. He was clearly irritated – as shown by his exchange with the guard. He was of quiet but nervous disposition and became flustered. He acted hurriedly 'without any thought or sense of responsibility'. Graham, the guard, had heard no belling when Hannah had gone into the box, although he had often heard the distinctive sound from the same position on other occasions. The fireman said that he had noticed Hannah using the bell when the train was about to move back over the crossover. It was likely that, as the District Controller had suggested: 'He had rushed into the box and possibly put his signals to danger before even touching his instruments. It seems like a temporary mental aberration.' He had not even sent the opening 5–5–5 signals to the other signalmen, let alone the 2–4 'Blocking Back Inside Home Signal', before letting the shunt begin. Most seriously, he had ignored the block instrument indications which would have given him the essential information and he had disregarded the fundamental principal that, unless he had actually seen it, a signalman must wait to receive the 'Out Of Section' before assuming that a particular train had passed.

Patently Hannah was not a man who should have been left in charge of a main line box – however little used it might be. He did not seem to understand the basic principles of block working. Yet he had passed examinations as recently as April and June so there was doubt as to whether or not the standards of selection and supervision in the District were all they should have been. That his inadequacies were not detected earlier in his career was much to be deplored.

In view of the fact that there had been such an extraordinarily good record in respect of the opening and closing of signal boxes, it was fair to assume that the Regulations were generally satisfactory. It was vital to ensure that they were both understood and observed, however, and beyond that there was little the Inspector could recommend to prevent anything of the sort happening again. There was clearly the need to employ only men of character, who could be implicitly relied upon, in the more responsible positions. The laxity in following regulations on the line generally was noted and Lt-Col Mount was reminded that similar disregard for other rules had been a major factor in an accident three years previously just a little way up the line on the other side of Langwathby.

In Waste Bank tunnel a five-vehicle local passenger train, headed by a 4–6–0 Claughton engine, had run head-on into a stationary ballast train which was loading spent ballast from the down track. The driver of the Claughton had died as had one of the passengers. The passenger train had actually been in the control of its fireman who was under instruction and had overlooked the starting signal at Culgaith station which had been at danger. His supervising driver had obviously failed to notice this. All would have been well if it had not been for the premature removal of the detonators protecting the ballast train. It was disregard of the regulation covering this factor that led to the crash which, being in a tunnel, was a pretty nasty affair and blocked the line for forty-eight hours. Shock absorbing buffers on some of the coaches, as at Little Salkeld, considerably lessened the effect on the passengers and their

universal use was urged once again.

Hannah was charged with the manslaughter of Driver Shaughnessy and was tried at Cumberland Assizes in Carlisle that October. The jury, however, took a lenient view of his misdemeanours and he was acquitted. Perhaps they felt that his conscience would provide greater punishment than any the court could impose.

For there to be two significant accidents at the same place – within ½ mile of each other – is by no means unique in railway history and there are several examples in these volumes, but for the same engine to be involved in both incidents *is*, I think, unique. Poor no. 1010 had at least that distinction to compensate for its strange and coincidental misfortune.

5
Lytham
(London Midland & Scottish Railway)

In the early years of railways there were many accidents due to the breaking of wheel tyres, which were usually of welded iron fixed on with rivets – unlike the modern steel rings which are shrunk onto the wheels. Improvements in tyre manufacture and attachment, together with the introduction of Mansell composite wheels on rolling stock, gradually reduced the frequency of these failures from more than 1,200 in 1880 down to an average seventy a year by the mid-'twenties. On 24 December 1874, when thirty-four died and many more were injured in a train crowded with people on their way to Christmas destinations, it was the last time for half a century that a tyre breakage would lead to a major disaster in Britain. Indeed, during the latter thirty years of that time no passenger had even been hurt on such account. At Shipton-on-Cherwell, between Oxford and Banbury, on that Christmas Eve in 1874, it was a tyre on an elderly four-wheeled passenger coach that fractured and caused the worst-ever accident on the Great Western.

Fifty years of progress, and the diligent work of the wheel-tapper, had no doubt banished the thought that such a thing might occur again.

But any complacency was shattered in 1924 when a locomotive tyre broke near Lytham St Annes.

Blackpool and its adjacent Fylde seaside resorts owe much to the railway for their growth and prosperity. The surviving rail services may bring only a relatively small proportion of today's holidaymakers, but in the 'twenties the train was still supreme and the dozen or so coastal resort stations thereabouts annually received the bulk of the area's life-blood. Thousands and thousands of suitcases, buckets and spades erupted onto the many platforms. Blackpool alone had five stations, and a halt, and Lytham St Annes had – and still has – three. Blackpool Central has now been erased and South Shore station and Burlington Road halt have closed. Waterloo Road is now called Blackpool South and is the terminus for the DMUs that still serve the southern Fylde branch through Lytham from Kirkham. The more important trains now run into Blackpool North in Talbot Road, from which it once took its name. There is a subsequently built station at Squires Gate to serve the Pontins Holiday Camp there, but the direct by-pass line from Waterloo

Road to Kirkham has long been dismantled.

Singled in 1983, with Moss Side station (a couple of miles before Lytham) re-opened after two decades at a cost to the county council of £7000, the line would seem to have at least an immediate future – despite its general air of dereliction. Today it has only a local shuttle service, but in the 'twenties it carried many through-trains and was comfortably prosperous.

On Monday 3 November 1924 the Blackpool Central part of the 4.40 pm Liverpool–Manchester and Blackpool express was on time and travelling at its usual speed towards Lytham, where it was due to call at 5.47. It had just run through Moss Side when the fireman, Livingstone, noticed sparks flying at the front end of the engine. He was about to tell his driver, Crookes, when it must have seemed that the end of the world had come and he blacked

12. Lytham. No. 1105 being lifted upright and out of the debris of the demolished Warton signal box and torn up track.

out. He awoke to find himself surrounded by steam and pinned under a fallen telegraph pole.

The sparks he had seen were from the engine's front bogie wheels which were off the metals and, when they encountered a rail that crossed the inner rail on which the train was running, the end was close at hand. This displaced the whole of the bogie which hit a girder on a bridge over a dyke a few yards further on and was wrenched away from its fastening. The engine, an ex-L and Y 4–4–0 no. 1105, left the track and the whole train, travelling at around 50 mph, was derailed with it. Warton signal box was just past this point and the engine hit and demolished it. The signalman was very lucky to escape with his life, though he was badly injured. Not so lucky were the driver and fourteen passengers. The train was fairly full and the first two coaches overturned, leading to the deaths and most of the serious injuries. Although the train was gas lit there was mercifully no fire on account of this – or the death toll would certainly have been much higher. A fire did develop from the burning coals in the signal box grate but this was quickly extinguished and no one suffered because of it.

The crossing rail, that had been struck by the derailed bogie wheel, led into the trailing points from Lytham Gas Works siding which was on the up side of the line. The proximity of the gas works proved a blessing once disaster had befallen, for the speed with which the rescue operation got under way was in no small measure due to an engineer at the works, a Mr Ranft, who had seen the crash from his office 600 yards away and had immediately sent his foreman to gather men and tools to provide prompt help whilst he phoned all the relevant services.

The engine and its six-wheeled tender ended up facing in the wrong direction on the embankment slope, the engine on its right side and the tender tilting that way. The two overturned carriages were further down beyond the tender and lying on the other track. Ninety yards of the down line was torn up by the crash, some of the rails being bent into a semi-circle.

Four hundred yards back up the line, in a field, was the tyre of no. 1105's left-hand leading bogie wheel. It was broken open and examination showed a large defect in the centre of the tread at the break. The opposite wheel also had a fractured tyre, but that had been caused by the violent impact after the derailment when it struck the crossing rail.

The tyres had been made at Horwich works and the faulty one was from a batch of thirty-four made and fitted four years previously. The engine had come out of Horwich only ten days before the accident, following general repairs which included turning up all the wheels – skimming about $3/16$ inch off them. The soundness of the tyres had been checked at that time as far as was possible. The failed tyre had travelled more than 100,000 miles on various engines over those previous four years, its time bomb of a flaw quite unsuspected. The remaining tyres from the batch that were still in use were replaced after the crash, and all thirty of them were broken up to look for similar deficiencies. None were found.

There were around 24,000 steam locomotives in use in Great Britain in 1924 and the average rate of tyre failure at that time, in relation to miles worked, was in the region of 1: 27,000,000. Add to this the fact that it was rare for a tyre to leave the wheel even when it did break and it will be appreciated just how freakish was this case.

In view of the facts in the matter, the Investigating Officer, our old friend Col J. W. Pringle, had few recommendations to make and no culprits to identify. For once there was no one to blame in any real sense. He suggested some technical improvements in the way tyres were handled by the works and urged research into practical means of detecting flaws in metal used to make such gear. He would certainly have been impressed with today's ultrasonic testing which can betray the tiniest flaw. Such developments were then still many years ahead.

Other than that, he expressed some surprise that the footplatemen had not noticed any difference in the way their engine negotiated the curve over which they were travelling when the bogie became derailed as the tyre flew off. The line was, however, notorious for giving a rough ride thereabouts and that may well have disguised any irregularity.

He mentioned, somewhat wearily and for the umpteenth time, the inherent danger of gas lighting on trains even though on this occasion no gas had ignited. The horrors of the gas-fed fires at Hawes Junction and Ais Gill, elsewhere on the Midland (then LMS) network, were no doubt in the forefront of his mind since he had presided over the inquiries into both those disasters. No gas-lit carriages were built by the

13. Lytham. Lowering the engine onto the undamaged up line. The angle of the shot highlights the absence of the four-wheeled bogie that was wrenched off. From this side the locomotive looks otherwise little damaged, the right-hand side having taken all the trauma.

Midland after Ais Gill in 1913, but many were still in use, and later at Charfield it was Midland stock – some of it more than forty years old – that featured in the last of the deadly gas-fed railway fires. He also drew attention to the Company's failure to provide rescue equipment on its non-corridor stock even where it was used for express services. If Mr Ranft and his well-equipped men had not been so fortuitously to hand, that could have been crucial. The Company was censured and the rescuers appropriately commended.

No villains here then. A hero or two, and some tragic bereavements, but none this time who would carry for the rest of their lives, as so many have had to do after other tragedies, the terrible knowledge that they were personally responsible for the deaths and injuries that occurred.

Lytham was the last instance of a broken tyre leading to death on a British train. By ingenuity and determination, a source of dangerous trouble that was once so common had – decades before today's advanced technology – been reduced to a level where it might occur, at most, once every 27 million miles.

6
Darlington
(London and North Eastern Railway)

This is the story of a young engine driver whose inexperience proved to be his undoing. There is more than one echo of the events at Ditton Junction sixteen years earlier in this tale, though there the misreading of signals led to derailment whilst here it resulted in collision with an innocent passing train.

Driver Hughes at Ditton had been a 'spare' driver; at Darlington the driver was actually a 'Passed Fireman' – meaning one who was qualified to drive but had not yet been upgraded. He was thirty-two and came from Gateshead; his name was Bell. He had done a good deal of the sort of driving a man in his position might expect: taking light engines to and from the sheds, working local freights and the like. On the Wednesday night in question, 27 June 1928, he was called upon to deputise for the regular man on a main line turn: the 9.30 pm semi-fast from Newcastle to Darlington, which continued as a parcels-only train to York. At Darlington it usually did some shunting to add or detach vehicles. Bell had travelled the road to York many times as fireman and once before as a driver. He had not been called upon to ac-

knowledge officially, by signing the road book, that he knew the line and signals, but he said that he had been quite prepared to do so. Knowledge of the road is one thing, however, and knowledge of the sidings quite another, and in all his journeys Bell had never had to shunt in Darlington station. As he put it himself: 'A man might go ten years between Newcastle and Darlington and know nothing of the "middle road".' The 'middle road' was the popular name for the line next to the platform line, more properly called the 'Up Duplicate'.

Darlington Bank Top station is looped off the main line to the west – the down side. It consists essentially of a wide island platform with a bay at the southern end and a dock at the northern one. The general layout of the tracks at the time that concerns us can be seen from the diagram. The 'back road' (or Up Siding, officially) was removed during resignalling in 1972, and there have been various other changes of detail, of course, but it is much the same today as it was then. The point of convergence of the back and middle roads with the platform one was only 48 yards from the junction with the main line at the

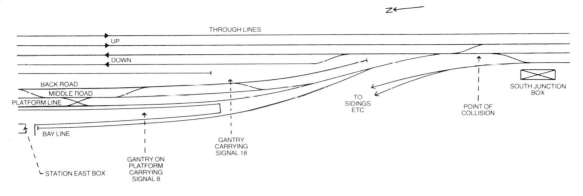

THROUGH LINES

UP

DOWN

BACK ROAD
MIDDLE ROAD
PLATFORM LINE

BAY LINE

STATION EAST BOX

GANTRY ON
PLATFORM
CARRYING
SIGNAL 8

GANTRY
CARRYING
SIGNAL 18

TO
SIDINGS
ETC

POINT OF
COLLISION

SOUTH JUNCTION
BOX

DARLINGTON · TRACK LAYOUT

south of the station, so lengthy trains wanting to shunt between any of the three tracks had to run out onto the main line.

On this night Bell reached Darlington at 10.45, eleven minutes late, in charge of ex-NER B16 class 4–6–0 no. 2369. He drew up at the north end of the platform, but was signalled forward to the south end to make room for another train. Standing in the middle road was a rake of seven vans, which were to be included in the train behind the third van. Shunter Morland uncoupled between the third and fourth vehicles and told Bell that he was to run up to the South Junction and back onto the middle road to pick up the seven vans. Since Bell had 45 yards of engine and vans, this meant running out onto the main line in order to clear the points and get back on to the platform road. In the normal course a simple forward-and-back shunt requires a single signal only, and so would this one have done if it had not involved fouling the main line. As it was, two signals were required. Directly ahead of Bell was the small calling-on signal No. 8 which gave him permission to move as far as signal No. 18, the middle road starter 100 yards ahead protecting the main line. Signal No. 8 was duly lowered, and Bell moved forward. But an excursion train from

Scarborough to Newcastle was due to pass on the down main line, so signal No. 18 remained at danger. Bell, however, had managed to convince himself that signal No. 8 gave him permission to complete his shunt, and though No. 18 was on a gantry of three, all at danger, he ran past it and on to the main line.

How did Bell come so to delude himself? He was at a loss to explain. Even granted his ignorance of the signalling, and if he was not quite certain which signal was his, it seems extraordinary that he should run past a group of three, all of them at danger. Looking back now, we can perhaps suggest how the confusion may have arisen in his mind. In the first place there was the unusual circumstance of a second signal being involved in the shunt. In the second place, while signal No. 8 was on Bell's right, the entire gantry on which No. 18 stood was on his left. With the back road on his left side also, and other lines beyond, he may have persuaded himself that none of the three referred to the middle road. Bell himself said that he was misled by a similar case of signalling at Newcastle, but this one turned out on examination to be different. It appeared, though, that other enginemen before Bell had found the signalling here confusing. A shouted explanation from the Station East signal

14. Darlington. No. 2164, of the excursion, lying minus its buffer beam where its journey had been so abruptly ended. Its detached tender, partially obscured by rising steam, is being lifted by the cranes.

box, close to which Bell's engine was standing, might have put things right, but signalmen were loath to trust a verbal message against the noise of the engines.

So Bell, in all innocence, was away out onto the main line. An alarmed Morland, riding on the third van, saw him pass signal No. 18 and lifted the brake tap in the van. Morland did not apply the brake fully, he explained, for fear of breaking the train. The train had slowed down to a walking pace when Morland heard a whistle. 'He's "got the boards",' he thought – clear signals – and released the brake. But he was wrong; it was the approaching excursion train which had whistled. He looked out again. He was nearly level with signal No. 18, which was still at danger. He applied the brake again, and had brought the train nearly to a standstill when the collision occurred.

Signalman Garrett in the South Junction box, all unaware of Bell's foray onto the main line, had set the road for the excursion. Then he heard a curious clicking noise in the level frame. It was Bell's train running through two sets of trailing points set against him. Garrett did not know this, but the noise meant something was amiss, and he threw the excursion's signals to danger. Too late.

Driver McNulty, in charge of ex-NER Z class Atlantic no. 2164, at the head of eleven coaches, was travelling at about 45 mph as he approached South Junction box. At the down home signals just beyond, he saw the lights of Bell's engine running in from the left onto his road – not more than 50 yards away. He reacted with lightning speed. With only two or three seconds to act he had no time to use sand or reverse his engine. He applied his Westinghouse brake, which was just beginning to bite when the two engines met head-on.

Bell had seen the lights of the excursion at just about the same time. He had the presence of mind to release his brakes in order to lessen the shock.

Bell's engine was driven back 60 yards along the down main line. It was not derailed, but it had its buffer beam knocked off and was otherwise badly damaged. The first four vans behind it were totally destroyed. No. 2164 of the excursion, likewise minus its buffer beam, ran forward for 65 yards before overturning on its left side, with its tender broken loose behind it. All the coaches of the excursion train remained upright, but the underframe of the third coach cut into five crowded compartments of the second – a non-corridor – and no one in these escaped death or injury.

Twenty-five passengers lost their lives; forty-five were seriously injured, as were the two drivers and also the fireman of the excursion. How Morland, riding on the third van, escaped death is a mystery.

Twenty of the dead were women, fourteen of them on a Mothers' Union outing from the colliery township of Hetton-le-Hole. To Hetton it was like a pit disaster with widowers instead of widows; there were four in a single street.

The inquiry, which was another conducted by Col Pringle, gave rise to one of the periodic flickers of animosity that have always been a feature of the relationship between the railway unions. The General Secretary of the locomotive men's union tried to put the responsibility for the accident onto Signalman Robson in the Station East box – a man with fifty years' experience who does not come into our story because he acted correctly throughout. Col Pringle would have none of it: 'There is no responsibility on this man,' he said.

The primary fault quite clearly lay with Bell. His knowledge of signalling, the Colonel concluded, was insufficient to enable him to read the signals of a strange yard correctly; he should have sought information from Morland. But Bell was commended for the straightforward way in which he had given his evidence. Morland had also had to bear a share of the blame, in that he should have acted more resolutely and applied the brake to the full when he saw Bell over-running the signal. Driver McNulty of the excursion train was absolved from all blame, as were all the signalmen concerned.

There was perhaps a point in Morland's defence that was not brought out at the inquiry. He must have known by heart the times of all the regular trains passing on the main line. If the excursion had been an ordinary scheduled train, Morland would have known it was due and would certainly have brought Bell to a stop. But he was not to know anything about a special.

As for signalling, Col Pringle suggested the substitution of a single three-aspect colour light signal for each of the three lines, which would show yellow when the signal ahead was at danger. Even the most inexperienced man could not possibly misunderstand this. In due course, eleven years later, this recommendation was carried out and the whole of Darlington station converted to colour light signalling.

15. Darlington. The two coaches in which most of the casualties occurred at the tragic conclusion to a seaside trip. The third-class ex-NER non-corridor coach (no. 2886) has been cut into by the underframe of the following ex-GCR composite corridor coach (no. 1304) during the rapid deceleration of the speeding train. The two carriages are largely superimposed, with the roof of the one lying on top on most of the roof of the other.

Illustrated London News

The Colonel also had a word to say about the value of buck-eye couplings in preventing telescoping. The LNER adopted these later as standard and their value is seen in other accidents dealt with in these volumes.

The year 1928 was the worst for accidents that the grouped Companies ever experienced. In thirteen of them there were fatalities and, in total, fifty-seven people died. One of the year's other major crashes also involved a shunting train – that was the one at Charfield mentioned in previous chapters and detailed in *Trains to Nowhere*. Just over the rump of the year, in

January 1929, there was yet another such collision. This, like Charfield, was on the LMS West of England line. At Ashchurch, near Tewkesbury, in the early hours of the morning, a Bristol–Leeds express hit a reversing goods train crossing from the up to the down line. The driver of the express, who was killed, over-ran the signals and it was thought that he must have missed the distant in a fog patch. The trains were heavily damaged but only three passengers died in the lightly loaded express.

Thrice within six months the same basic ingredients of disaster. The details differed, the blame was variously allocated, but one ringing fact emerged from the inquiries held: all three could have been prevented with Automatic Train Control. Yet its general application was still nearly thirty years away.

7
Friog
(Great Western Railway)

Most landslips on railways are trivial affairs and, although they cause some disruption to services on occasion, they rarely lead to accidents. There are exceptions though, as illustrated in the Little Salkeld chapter, and two other such exceptions, which occurred in the same 900 yards of track as each other, led to the name of Friog being added to that curious list of places where the lightning of bad luck has struck twice.

Pronounced as in the anglicised spelling 'Vriog', it was originally in Merionethshire but is now in the new Welsh county of Gwynedd. It is principally the name of a hamlet and lies between Llwyngwril and Fairbourne where the Cambrian Coast line hugs the very edge of Britain. It never merited so much as a halt, but it did lend its name to a cutting. It should ideally have lent it to something more substantial.

Winding up the coastline from Aberystwyth to Pwllheli, out on the remote Lleyn peninsular, the line was built by the under-financed Cambrian Railway Company between 1862 and 1865. Every effort was made to cut costs to the minimum and where a tunnel could be avoided by making a cutting, however preferable the former would have been, a cutting there was. Friog was such an example and the single line was cut ninety feet above the sea along the side of the Cader Idris mountain range.

In the first couple of decades there were no serious problems there, but in the exceptionally wet winter that began in 1882 the inherent weakness of the earthwork became tragically apparent. On the evening of the first day of January 1883 the engine and tender of a passenger train were swept over the cliff and plunged down onto the beach below. The driver and fireman were killed. They had run into the start of a landslide in which more than 100 tons of peaty loam and stones, the latter from a retaining wall, came down and covered the line.

The engine was a 2–4–0 no. 29, 'Pegasus', and it was surprisingly little damaged despite being hurled onto the rocky foreshore. It was recovered and repaired and ran for another thirty years. The passengers were very lucky to escape serious injury as the leading coach was dragged after the locomotive; however, the coupling to the tender broke and the carriage was left overhanging the cliff. The second coach overturned but ended up in a safer position, and

Railway Disaster Follows Snow in Merioneth.

Engine Driver and Fireman Hurled to Death.

LOCOMOTIVE CRASHES OVER CLIFF

PASSENGER'S GRAPHIC STORY

The picturesque coastline of Merioneth with its rugged cliffs overlooking Cardigan Bay was the scene in the early hours of Saturday of a distressing railway disaster, caused by an extensive landslide, and resulting in the deaths of an engine driver and fireman.

Mr. John Humphreys (58), the driver was a married man with two children, and his home was at Tanrallt-street, Machynlleth. The fireman, Mr. J. P. Kenny (28), a native of Pwllheli, also lived at Machynlleth—in Maglona Villas. In order that he might visit his mother, who is lying ill at Pwllheli, Mr. Kenny, a married man with no children, asked another fireman, Mr. Tom James, Pennal, if he would change periods of duty with him on the fateful morning, and Mr. James agreed to do so.

Leaving Machynlleth at 5.10 a.m., the train concerned, carrying one passenger, a guard, and an assistant guard, proceeded on its way along the curved railroad by the side of the cliff, until it reached Friog, a cutting between Llwyngwril and Fairbourne, where the disaster occurred. The couplings connecting the engine and the first coach snapped, and the locomotive was hurled over a wall nearly five feet high, and dashed on to the rocks below, the driver and fireman having no possible opportunity of saving themselves.

The breaking of the couplings undoubtedly saved the lives of the passenger, guard, and assistant guard. The first coach was derailed, but stayed on the permanent way, all the other coaches remaining on the metals.

News of the catastrophe soon spread and assistance summoned. Railwaymen, police, Dr. J. R. Heath, Barmouth, and others were quickly on the scene. Much difficulty was experienced in extricating the bodies of the driver and fireman, the rescue party having to work against the tide. The bodies were conveyed to the top of the precipice at about 10 a.m. and were taken to Llwyngwril Railway Station where the Merioneth Coroner (Mr. R. Guthrie Jones, Dolgelley) opened an inquest. After evidence of identification, however, had been given the proceedings were adjourned until March 14th, when the inquest will be resumed at Barmouth.

A gang of men were promptly engaged to clear the rails. G.W.R. officials have visited the scene and held a private inquiry on Tuesday morning. It was hoped to have the railroad passable by mid-day on Thursday, when an inquiry into the disaster was held at Llwyngwril on behalf of the Board of Trade.

PASSENGER'S THRILL.

RUSH TO FAIRBOURNE FOR ASSISTANCE.

Guard and Assistant's Ordeal.

Thousands of people made the journey to Friog on Saturday and Sunday to see the terrible destruction, and daily newspapers succeeded in taking remarkable photographs from aeroplanes.

Passenger's Story.

Mr. Ronald Goodsell, 5, Cambrian-terrace, Towyn, the only passenger on the train, is a son of Mr. and Mrs. Goodsell, Gas Works, Dolgelley, and is engaged as mechanic in connection with Dolgelley, Barmouth, and Towyn Gas Works. In an interview with "The Cambrian News" representative at Dolgelley, Mr. Ronald Goodsell explained that he left Towyn by the 6.35 a.m. mail train on Saturday for Dolgelley where a big contract was on hand to repair a gasometer. "I generally travel in the carriage next to the engine," added Mr. Goodsell, "but on this occasion I chose

THE ENGINE DRIVER.

The Late Mr. John Humphreys.

the third and last carriage because that happened to have a corridor.

"After leaving Llwyngwril Station, Mr. Dick Lewis, an assistant guard, entered my compartment and we discussed Aberystwyth Town's football prospects. While we were thus chatting, there was a severe bumping, like what might be caused by a smash, though it did not resemble thunder or an explosion as was stated in some newspapers. On seeing the guard's door open, we both hastened thither and found the guard (Mr. Edward Humphreys, Machynlleth), applying the brakes. Guard Humphreys remarked tragically 'The engine has gone to the bottom' and then went to a telephone call-box on the side of the line with the intention of sending an S.O.S.; but the wires had been broken. The guard thereupon hastened on foot to Llwyngwril."

Almost Blinded by Steam.

Mr. Goodsell described how he descended the slope by means of a chain used by platelayers and added:

"On reaching the spot where the engine lay, the steam almost blinded me. However, I saw the bodies of the engine driver and fireman. They were both dead."

"As nothing further could be done then," concluded Mr. Goodsell, "I called out to Mr. Dick Lewis that I would report the matter. I walked along the foreshore to Fairbourne and then to Barmouth Junction, where I caught the train which reached Dolgelley at 8.10 a.m." Mr. Goodsell emphasised that he did not see the engine go over the cliff.

Prayer For Passenger's Safety.

Mrs. Goodsell, the mother of Mr. Ronald Goodsell, is assistant organist at Dolgelley Church, and his sister (Mrs. Wynne Thomas) is honorary secretary of the women's section of the British Legion and of the Nursing Association. On Sunday the Rev. Dr. J. W. James, rector of Dolgelley, offered a prayer of thanks for the safety of Mr. Goodsell. For over two years Mr. Goodsell was on active service in France during the Great War and sustained shell-shock. A week prior to the train accident he was travelling by train from Towyn and had to get out of his compartment and walk back home owing to a snowdrift at Tonfanau.

Heard an Explosion.

Mr. Richard J. Lowe, Derwenlas, porter-signalman, acting as assistant guard on the train, told a "Cambrian News" reporter he was travelling in the same compartment as Mr. Goodsell, when he heard something like a shot from a gun. He looked out on the cliff side, but could see nothing as the train was on a bend. Proceeding to ascertain from Guard Humphreys what happened, he was informed that the engine had "gone over."

"I then went with Mr. Goodsell to the landslide," Mr. Lewis further stated.

"There was no trace of the engine driver or of the fireman. I went over the side of the cliff by means of an emergency chain; but there was too much steam for me to go near the engine. I heard an explosion at the bottom of the cliff and finding it impossible to do anything I returned to the train. Mr. Goodsell went to give information at Fairbourne."

The train was due at Barmouth at 7.15 a.m. and was only a few miles away when the calamity occurred. Dr. J. R. Heath, Barmouth, and railway officials, were taken to the scene by a special engine. The Doctor descended the cliff, but found he could do nothing for the driver or fireman, both, apparently, having been killed instantaneously.

ENGINE WRECKED.

INQUEST ON VICTIMS OPENED.

Coroner Adjourns Proceedings.

After a rush against the incoming tide the bodies of the two men were recovered and removed to Llwyngwril Station, where Mr. Guthrie Jones, Dolgelley, the coroner for Merioneth, opened an inquest on Saturday evening. The Coroner said evidence of identification only would be taken that evening so that burial of the bodies could take place.

Evidence of identification was given by Mr. James Banks, locomotive engineer, Machynlleth. It was stated that Mr. Kenny had changed duty with another fireman so that he might visit his mother who was ill at Pwllheli.

The inquest was adjourned until March 14th, when it will be resumed at Barmouth at 2.30 p.m.

Total Wreck.

It is understood that the engine and

THE FIREMAN.

The Late Mr. J. P. Kenny.

tender, which lay totally wrecked on the foreshore, will be dismantled and removed at the earliest possible opportunity.

A section of the main road above the railway, where the accident occurred, is badly damaged and closed to traffic. Part of the boundary wall on the main road, tons of earth, huge pieces of rock and slate have fallen on to the rails and gangs of men have been hard at work, day and night, to get the permanent way clear, which, it was hoped, would be so at midday on Thursday.

Workmen Tied to Ropes.

To safeguard the men working on the cliff below the main road, which is now closed to traffic, skilled rockmen, tied to long ropes firmly fastened to iron bars driven into a safe portion of the road, were employed to dislodge loose stones.

Traffic Diverted.

Since the rails have been impassable, traffic between Dovey Junction to Barmouth Junction has been suspended, the trains being diverted from Dolgelley to Machynlleth along Talyllyn mountain pass. Buses have conveyed passengers from Machynlleth through Corris and Dolgelley, for Barmouth direction.

Similar Disaster.

At the same spot fifty-one years ago a similar disaster occurred. A train fell into the sea, carrying with it the driver and fireman, both of whom were killed. On that occasion the passengers were returning from the afternoon session of Eisteddfod Meirion, and when the news was received at the hall in the evening the Eisteddfod was abandoned.

The above remarkable photograph gives a bird's eye view of the landslide. The section of the wall over which the engine was hurled on to the rocks on the foreshore below is seen covered by debris.

"DAILY EXPRESS" ENTERPRISE.

The photographs reproduced on this page of the landslide and of the two unfortunate victims were kindly lent to "The Cambrian News" through the courtesy of "The Daily Express" whose enterprise resulted in that journal publishing what was freely described as the best picture of the disaster.

SOCIAL AND PERSONAL.

The Prince of Wales has consented to attend the Derby Ball, which Lady Milbanke is arranging at Grosvenor House on Tuesday, May 30.

Looking exceedingly fit and sunburnt after his successful safari in the Sudan (cables Reuter), the Duke of Gloucester arrived at Port Said on Monday afternoon on board the liner Gloucestershire.

Capt. R. T. Evans, M.P., who is suffering from a severe cold at his home in Llandaff, was unable to preside at the Carmarthen Drama Festival on Saturday.

Mr. D. Owen Evans, M.P., and Mrs. Evans, will leave London on Thursday for America on the Aquitania. They will be away for about a month.

Nine prisoners were convicted and three acquitted in the Liverpool riots case.

It is feared that the earthquake and tidal wave disaster in Japan has caused 3,000 casualties. The latest figures give the number of dead as more than 1,500 and the missing as nearly 1,500.

VIGILANT GANGER.

SAVES DANGEROUS SITUATION AT ABERDOVEY.

A G.W.R. ganger (Mr. Hughes, Aberdovey), patrolling his length on Tuesday morning noticed a fall of earth and rubble at a spot approximately 200 yards east of Picnic Island, a mile out of Aberdovey. Mr. Hughes hurried to the station to report the matter, and a gang was promptly on the scene. An inspection revealed that an old wall which lines the main road which runs parallel to the railway had cracked and was giving way, the lose earth at its base being precipitated to a spot several yards clear of the railway track thirty feet below.

None of the debris touched the track; and undoubtedly the fact that the "slide" was noticed in time saved what might have developed into a dangerous situation. On Tuesday afternoon sightseers from the town watched U.D. Council workmen erecting a barrier to protect the cracked wall.

Our reporter was informed at Aberdovey station that there was no danger, though trains were being warned to proceed cautiously. There has been no further fall of earth. The main road is quite clear for traffic, and the train service normal. It is surmised that the fall was caused by vibration due to heavy road traffic, coupled with the effect of the recent heavy snowstorm. It is estimated that the actual fall of rubble would be about four or five hundredweights only.

the remaining coach, which luckily contained most of the modest complement of passengers, stayed with the brake van on the rails. The engine crew were the only fatalities.

Colonel Rich, at the ensuing inquiry, considered that the slip could probably not have been foreseen and was the result of the unusually heavy falls of snow and rain over the preceding weeks. He accepted that the ideal technical solution to the problem of avoiding a recurrence, that of substituting a tunnel, was not a realistic one in view of the line's fragile financial viability. He therefore suggested, as a compromise, that the roadway that ran 100 feet above the track should be better drained and maintained, and that there should be a 4 mph speed limit for trains passing through the cutting to reduce the chances of vibration starting a slide. The stretch should also be carefully watched.

His recommendations were adopted, but by the end of the century the road had been improved and heavy rails laid on the railway so the speed restriction was relaxed to 8 mph. With no further trouble, by 1923 it was up to 15 mph. When the GWR took over the Company at the Grouping, it did what it could to drag the Cambrian's routes up towards its own high standards, but the coastal line was never a money-spinner and was almost as vulnerable to pruning then as it is now. It did not justify major expenditure, though quite a lot of work was done and Friog cutting got something of a face-lift in the process.

16 (*opposite*). Friog, 1933. *Daily Express* pictures of the landslide, and the crew of the engine, reproduced here in a page from the local weekly. The whole course of the slide can be clearly followed from the roadway above down to the heap of debris on the foreshore below. There are many interesting details contained in the accompanying copy – for those who care to fetch a magnifying glass! Note the item in the bottom right-hand corner about another landslip from similar causes at Aberdovey. Above it is a reference to the 1883 incident.

By 1930 the degree to which the cutting was watched had been reduced to the norm for all such earthworks, and the drama of New Year's Day 1883 had been essentially forgotten. Then it happened again.

This time there was a prologue. On 24 February 1933, a train was blocked by snow there and a snow plough had to be called out. A snow drift of this kind was most unusual on a coastal line but no one saw it as the prelude it was to the disaster that was to come only eight days later.

On Saturday 4 March, the 6.10 am mail train from Machynlleth to Pwllheli (which was again a train consisting of three coaches, though with a milk van in rear this time) was passing through the cutting at the now permitted speed of 15 mph just after 7.5 am. The reverberation its passage created was the trigger that the vengeful mountain was awaiting, and 2,000 tons of loose stone and earth, including a considerable length of the roadway's retaining wall, cascaded down onto the front of the train. It was just ½ mile south of the previous slip which had happened almost exactly fifty years before.

In an eerie reconstruction of history, the locomotive and its tender were once more swept over the cliff onto the seashore below and the crew killed. Again the rest of the rolling stock was spared and no one else seriously hurt. Indeed, this time the rest of the train was hardly damaged at all. The scene, unlike 1883, was in daylight, but in all essential respects it could hardly have been much more of a repeat performance of the original drama.

The engine, an ex Cambrian 0–6–0 no. 874, was less lucky than its predecessor, however. It was completely wrecked and cut up where it lay, to be hauled away as scrap.

On this occasion the Inspecting Officer, Lt-Col Mount, did not think that there had been sufficient surface water to cause the slide and concluded that the cause was the gradual, but by then considerable, increase in road traffic on the A493 above the line. A particularly heavily laden lorry had passed along the road on the previous day and this could well have had a decisive effect on the weakened substructure of the road. A crack in the road where the slip had started had been observed that evening by a couple of young pedestrians, but they had not thought it to be of urgent importance and had not reported it.

If the line was to have a future, and the ideal answer to the problem of Friog – a tunnel – was now even more uneconomic than it had been in the past, then the road would have to be cut further back into the headland and the slope between it and the railway would in some way need to be made more safe.

Now, another half-century on, trains still run through the cutting, but are no longer threatened. The road was realigned as recommended and, most significantly, an avalanche shelter – the only one in Britain – was built over the most vulnerable 200 feet of the track. Moreover, to guard against subsidence of the permanent way itself, huge concrete buttresses with steel reinforcement were built to support the cliff below the line.

The two engines tossed like toys from Friog cutting not only represent one of the strangest of railway coincidences; they are reminders of how resentful the hills and mountains can be of the presumptuous strips of steel that burrow and slice their way through and over the landscape.

Little Salkeld and Friog have both been the sites of landslip accidents, but the arbitrary link of coincidence between the Cumbrian and the Cambrian places is actually fourfold. Each has seen two significant accidents; each pair of accidents occurred ½ mile apart and the second one in each case happened in 1933. Of no significance, of course, it is perhaps a curiosity of some passing interest.

8
Welwyn Garden City
(London & North Eastern Railway and Eastern Region, BR)

On more than one occasion we may suspect that if the man in the signal box had been a bit brighter or more alert there would have been no disaster. It is rare, however, for it to be said officially that he should not have been assigned to the post. But that is what was said by Lt-Col Mount at Little Salkeld in 1933 and, only two years later, he found himself repeating the same sentiment about another signalman.

Signalman Fred Howes was no novice. He had had twenty-three years' experience and Welwyn Garden City was his fourth box. It was also the first Class 1 box he had been given, but he had been chosen for it by seniority rather than merit. The stationmaster there described him as 'an almost peculiarly quiet man; difficult to get anything out of him', while his instructor had noted that he had taken five weeks to learn the working of the box.

Welwyn Garden City signal box stood at the northern end of the down island platform and was an unusually busy one. The four-track main line was flanked on either side by the single-line branches to Luton and Hertford. The branches had their junction point with the main line at the next station up, Hatfield, but did not part company from it until the down side of Welwyn Garden City station. This meant that the box controlled three routes and six running tracks. The branch lines have no bearing on our story, but they meant that Welwyn (as it shall be referred to) was a box requiring a man who could be more than usually depended upon to keep his head at busy times. Howes was not such a man.

He had not been in the box on his own for a week before he was in trouble. It was quite a small incident: he had pulled off the inner home signal too soon and allowed a driver to over-run the outer home at danger. It would have passed off with a mild reproof, but Howes got in touch with the driver to persuade him to help hush it up. When it came to light, and the stationmaster ordered him to make a report, he refused. So he found himself on the carpet at King's Cross, not for the original error but for indiscipline. He received a severe reprimand which was entered in his record. Confirmation of the reprimand was awaiting him in the box

59

when he came on duty for the ten o'clock shift on the night of 15 June 1935. Whether the state of mind it engendered had any effect on his actions just over an hour later can only be conjectured, but it is at least possible that brooding resentment helped to take his mind off his work. It was not the most tactful of times to deliver such a document to a signalman.

The 10.45 pm King's Cross–Newcastle was being run in two parts. The first train reporting, no. 825, left at the scheduled time. The second part, no. 825A, which was to take the coastal route via Sunderland, left at 10.53, well filled on that Saturday night with 280 passengers. It was hauled by one of the famous C1 class Ivatt Atlantics, no. 4441. Behind it, at 10.58, came train no. 826, the newspaper express to Leeds due away at 10.50. It had three passenger coaches amongst its eleven vehicles, carrying fifty-seven passengers, and was headed by 2–6–0 no. 4009, one of Gresley's powerful K3 class, with nearly double the Atlantic's traction though not weighing a great deal more.

Train no. 825 ran through Welwyn and Howes sent the 'Train Out Of Section' back to Hatfield No. 3 box at 11.20 pm. Signalman Crowe had been working at Hatfield for eighteen of his thirty-four years with the Company. The trains had been bunching up somewhat and Crowe had already been offered train no. 825A from Hatfield No. 1 box. He offered it forward to Howes who accepted it forthwith. Crowe sent him 'Train Entering Section' for train no. 825A as it passed by at 11.22.

A moment later the phone from the station rang in Welwyn box. It was the porter on duty asking if Howes had phoned Hatfield about a parcel left in a train from Hertford. He had asked him earlier to make the call, which apparently he was unable to do himself. Since Howes had already had 'Train Entering Section' for train no. 825A he should have pulled off his signals for it, but for some reason – cussedness perhaps? – he made the call about the parcel first. In consequence he was late in clearing the signals and Driver Morris on the engine of train no. 825A, seeing the distant at caution, supposed that he was closing up on train no. 825. He shut off steam and applied the brakes. He had reduced speed to about 15 mph when he saw the home signal go off as Howes tardily got down to pulling his levers. Still assuming that he was on the heels of the first Newcastle train, Morris allowed himself only to roll on towards the starter. Seeing that it was clear he popped his whistle and put on steam again. Almost immediately he felt a violent impact as train no. 826 crashed into the rear.

Back to Crowe in Hatfield No. 3 box at 11.23. To his surprise, Crowe received the 'Train Out Of Section' from Howes for train no. 825A. It had apparently covered the 2½-mile section in one minute! Hatfield No. 1 box had just offered train no. 826 to Crowe and he offered it on to Howes who accepted it at once. Signalman Crowe was not happy. It all seemed to him to be 'a bit smart', as he put it later, so he picked up the phone and asked Howes: 'Is that out, Fred?' 'Yes,' came the reply. The Leeds train, no. 826, went past his box at 11.25 and he sent 'Train Entering Section' to Welwyn. At 11.29 he received 'Danger Obstruction' from Howes. Crowe picked up the phone again. What was going on? '826 has run into the rear of 825A' Howes told him. 'But,' said Crowe, 'you gave "Train Out Of Section" for 825A at 11.23.' There was no reply.

Howes had wrongly checked one train,

17 (*opposite*). Welwyn Garden City, 1935. The recovery crane at work on the eighth vehicle of the Leeds train. It had partially telescoped into the one in front before turning over onto its side. Some of the newspaper vans, with their wooden bodies and frames, are standing at the northern end of the up platform (top right-hand corner of picture) having already been cleared from the running lines. Presiding over the scene is the signal box that was the centre of the developing drama.

18. Welwyn Garden City, 1935. The seventh coach of the Leeds train in a closer shot showing clearly the effect of the partial telescoping. Built in 1907, it is a composite brake (no. 43062) with a wooden body on a steel frame and screw couplings. Above the front of it can be glimpsed the signal gantry carrying, on the right, the starter that stood at danger, as it does now, in the face of the K3, but too late for its warning to have any effect. The home signal at the other end of the station had showed clear until the moment before the engine passed it, and only 400 yards remained before the end of the Newcastle train.

wrongly given 'Line Clear' and wrongly accepted another – all in the space of a few minutes. No wonder the Inspecting Officer thought him unsuitable for his post!

Let us go back now to the last moments before the collision. Driver Barnes, on the K3 hauling train no. 826 on its way to Leeds, was going well, climbing the 1 in 200 gradient towards Welwyn at 65 mph. The signals showed a beckoning green. But just as he came to the Welwyn home signal it changed to red. Beyond it Barnes saw the tail light on train no. 825A no more than 400 yards ahead. There was too little time to take effective action and the trains collided at a net speed of around 50 mph. The results were as spectacular as they were horrific. The K3 drove right through the last coach of the Newcastle train so that the frame of the carriage was festooned about the engine. The coach bogies, and those of the coach in front of it, were driven forward 140 yards. No one in the last coach survived. Strangely, many of the injured were found to be coated with a black grime which even ether could not remove. Its source was never established.

Despite the force of the impact, the K3 kept the rails. This probably did much to limit the damage to its train, but undoubtedly the principal factor in keeping the death toll of such a violent collision so low was the number of buck-eye couplings in use on both trains. Of the 300 people aboard them, only fourteen were killed – a remarkably low percentage. In the seven years since Darlington, the LNER had taken heed of the Inspector's advice concerning the use of these couplings and the benefit was now dramatically demonstrated. In train no. 825A the penultimate coach was an all-steel vehicle fitted with buck-eye couplings and shock-absorbing buffers. Despite having its bogies pushed forward the coupling in front held fast and supported the body so that no one in it was seriously injured.

In train no. 826 the contrast between the two types of coupling was remarkable. The first three vehicles had buck-eye couplings, all of which held. The leading vehicle, a van, partially telescoped into the tender, but in the second one there was not even a pane of glass broken. Though the couplings in the third vehicle held, a number of passengers in it were seriously injured, doubtless by the shock of the impact. The next six coaches, with ordinary screw couplings, were wrecked, but the last two with buck-eyes were not damaged. There could

hardly have been a more effective demonstration of the advantages of using the buck-eye type.

Clearly the accident had been due to Howes wrongly accepting the Leeds train. What had happened, it transpired at the inquiry, was that he had got mixed up between the two Newcastle trains. He had forgotten that he had already given 'Train Out Of Section' for train no. 825 at 11.20 and had imagined that the train he accepted at 11.23 was train no. 825A. There was no entry in his train book for the acceptance of train no. 826. He had been passing an up train at the same time and Lt-Col Mount thought that he had got thoroughly confused and had been giving and receiving signals and pegging trains on the wrong set of instruments. Thus he may have cleared the down block instrument for an up train

But Howes was far from playing the penitent's role. He tried to throw blame on to

19. Welwyn Garden City, 1935. A night photograph taken soon after the collision showing the comparatively little damaged engine of the second train, no. 826, entwined with the wreckage of the Newcastle train, no. 825A.

Illustrated London News

20. Welwyn Garden City, 1957. In this remarkable picture of the express, the derailment is seen as if in frozen motion. The last remaining coach (the other four having been hauled away) is sitting quite normally on the rails, whilst in front of it the train is in increasing degrees of displacement until at the front lies the prostrate locomotive.

Crowe, which we may think was wholly in character. In the face of the evidence he maintained that his 'Train Out Of Section' signal had referred to no. 825 and he had thought, therefore, that that was the one that Crowe was inquiring about when he had asked: 'Is that out?' The inspector was not impressed.

In his conclusions, Lt-Col Mount identified a weakness in the application of track circuits that was to have far-reaching results and make the

Welwyn accident of 1935 a key event in the progress of railway safety. Train no. 825A had not reached the track circuit that ran for 200 yards in rear of the home signal when the second acceptance was given – the one for train no. 826. The collision could have been prevented if the controls had been arranged so that once 'Line Clear' had been transmitted it could not have been sent again until the track circuit had been occupied and cleared. This system was so obviously desirable that it was widely adopted, particularly by the LNER, and became known as the 'Welwyn Control'.

Thus something good came out of the horror

– no thanks to Howes. The railways were becoming increasingly sensitive to the need to take very seriously the recommendations made by accident investigators and the contribution to safety for which these men have been responsible can hardly be overstated. They have often been able to point out inherent weaknesses in procedures and equipment and thus cause them to be eliminated. Not always, as we have seen elsewhere, has their advice been taken so readily as it was after this inquiry.

The Welwyn Control was a 'witness' in many a subsequent accident investigation and, by another of those strange haphazard flukes, one such inquiry concerned once more the place from which it had received its name. Twenty-two years later, on 7 January 1957, Welwyn Garden City signal box was again the focal point of events culminating in a collision where, as before, one train ran at speed into the back of another.

Class A2/3 Pacific no. 60520, 'Owen Tudor', hauling the Sunday night express from Aberdeen to King's Cross, ran into the rear of the 6.18 am Baldock–King's Cross local which was headed by an L1 class 2–6–4 tank engine, no. 67741. The slow train, which was running eleven minutes late, had just departed the up local platform. It was booked to run fast to Finsbury Park and so was admitted to the up fast line by way of the crossover just past the southern end of the station. It had accelerated to just over 30 mph, and gone about ½ mile, when the express, travelling at over 60 mph, caught it up and ploughed into the end of it. The last carriage of the six-coach local, a corridor brake-third, was wrecked and overturned. Even the presence of buck-eye couplings could not, in the circumstances, help the corridor-first coach next to it and that also overturned. The Pacific heading the express ended up on its side as well but was remarkably little damaged. The leading six

of the eleven coaches behind it were derailed but, in this case, the buck-eyes stopped them turning over and held them in good line so that their all-steel bodies were little affected. Most of the serious injuries, and the one death, were therefore in the end of the other train. Unfortunately the brake-second was running with the passenger section at the tail end, due to the after-effects of abnormal stock working over the Christmas holidays, and this fact was strongly criticised at the inquiry.

The culprit at this second Welwyn disaster was not the signalman but the driver of the express. Driver Knapp, who was only superficially hurt in the crash, was a last-minute substitute for the scheduled man who had been late reporting for duty. He had been at the New England depot in Peterborough for nearly thirty years, but, although he was fifty-nine, he had been qualified as a driver for only twelve. His experience of driving fast passenger trains was limited, and his knowledge of the route south of Hitchin was more from his years as a fireman than from the few trips he had made over that part of the road at the controls.

After passing through Welwyn North, he either misread, or simply missed, the outer distant signal at danger. His fireman, Tyers, was not assisting him in his observation of signals as he should have been. It was misty and only just beginning to dawn and the signal in question was just under the Welwyn North starter which was at clear and showing a green aspect. On his own admission he had only glanced at it. In any event, he passed the distant at danger and then failed to observe any of the subsequent four signals, all at danger, over the 1¾ miles into the next section.

The Inspector, Lt-Col G. R. S. Wilson, was at a loss to explain such a lapse but laid the blame for the accident fully on his shoulders. Here was a classic case where Automatic Train Control

21. Welwyn Garden City, 1957. A close-up of the Pacific as it lay shortly after the crash. The force of the collision is dramatically illustrated by the extent to which the front of the engine has caved in and the extent to which the track on which it was travelling has been distorted.

would have saved the day, but British Railways had only had the go ahead from the government in the previous year for their 'Automatic Warning System' and it was still in the trial stage. Ironically it was on trial on this very stretch of track and was installed at distant signals on the main running lines – including the Welwyn ones. But comparatively few engines were fitted

with the receiving equipment and, as fate would have it, the Pacific in question was not one of them.

The Lieutenant-Colonel had to contend with a good deal of apparent mendacity from witnesses as Knapp sought to establish some kind of mitigating circumstances that might help to excuse his behaviour. The signalman, on duty in the box where Howes had made his disastrous mistake a couple of decades earlier, was able to show – thanks to the Welwyn Control that was

22. Welwyn Garden City, 1957. Looking the other way, towards London, the wrecked rear of the local can be seen – the torn off rear bogie from the last coach lying by the express loco in the right-hand foreground. The crew of the V2 2–6–2 on the passing train look on – no doubt contemplating that 'there but for the grace of God . . .'

Popperfoto

Howes' involuntary bequest – that he could not have changed his mind, as was inferred at one stage, and altered the signals *after* the express had passed the outer distant.

So, by one of those quirks that fate seems to be so fond of providing, the Welwyn Control, born of a signalman's inadequacy, came to the aid of another signalman in the same box. One way and another, Welwyn is well entrenched in railway history.

The signal box has gone now and the semaphores have given way to colour lights remotely controlled from King's Cross. The Hertford branch is truncated just outside the town at Norton Abrasives' factory, and the freight contract there was lost in 1981 so even that is disused. The Luton branch has disappeared completely, though where it used to curve away westwards there are nine new sidings which accommodate the electric stock that provides the recently introduced service to Moorgate. Using the old Luton line platform as its terminus, the service runs through the old Northern City Underground tunnels at the other end of its route south from Finsbury Park – thus at last fulfilling the original intention of the GNR subsidiary that built them. Across the island platform at Welwyn, other 'Great Northern Electrics' from King's Cross run on to Royston. The overhead catenary will ultimately stretch up to Huntingdon and Peterborough – and even further north if British Rail gets its way.

Welwyn Garden City continues to be a busy location with several freight sidings still in use at the station and, to cater for the new electric trains, there is a flyover at the southern end to carry stock across the main line to the up side. Inter-City 125s now dash along that main line to provide the principal express services to and from the North and Scotland in place of the Atlantics, Pacifics and K3s of 1935 and 1957. The detail has changed markedly, but Welwyn is still very firmly on the railway map and seems likely to remain so. Its history has been touched by tragedy more than most, but, with any luck, the many modern improvements will keep it free of such sadness in the years ahead.

9
Shrivenham
(Great Western Railway)

Time and again have Investigating Officers pleaded the case for the widespread introduction of Automatic Train Control (ATC) and track circuits, pointing out that such equipment would have prevented, or at least lessened, the accident under consideration. Yet such highly desirable devices are still no guarantee, as we have seen, against that commonest of all disaster factors: human error. The Great Western had been in the forefront with ATC at distant signals, and also had put in a large number of track circuits. Both these features were present at Shrivenham in 1936, but that did not prevent an express running into the back of a freight train in the freezing darkness of a winter's morning.

Shrivenham is on the Wiltshire borders of Oxfordshire, some six miles east-north-east of Swindon. Before the 1974 boundary changes it was in neighbouring Berkshire; a more significant change to its status, some thought, happened ten years earlier when its station closed. The line is, of course, still very much in use, being the main route from London to Bristol and South Wales. Inter-City 125s speed past its desolate platforms now, keeping well away from them on the realigned double track.

But in 1936 the station had not long been rebuilt and the new platforms set back to accommodate four tracks and enable stopping trains to pull off the main line. The London-bound platform loop was extended to begin an up goods line which continued eastwards for 3 miles. There were two signal boxes, both of the latest GWR type with mechanical frames. Shrivenham box itself was just past the western end of the down platform, while 2/3 mile away at the eastern approach was Ashbury Crossing box.

The station buildings and the signal boxes have long gone, and even the level crossing by the Ashbury one has been removed; the lane it served coming now to an abrupt end on either side of the line. A road freight company uses the old goods yard as a depot, a sign of the times to be seen at many another abandoned station.

Let us travel back now, though not by road or rail but in time – half a century of time – to the beginning of 1936. It was 15 January but dawn was still some way off. It was a bitter black night with a hoar frost and low-lying patchy mist. The line then served the South-West peninsula and the overnight London express had left Penzance at 9 pm the previous evening. At

Newton Abbot, as usual, the engine had been changed. On this occasion it was King class no. 6007, 'King William III', that came on with Driver E. A. Starr and Fireman J. H. Cozens aboard. The run from there had been quite satisfactory and the nine-coach train had left Swindon punctually at 5.15 am. Visibility was none too clear but not bad enough to justify getting fogmen out. They were still accelerating and travelling at about 50 mph when they heard the clear signal bell on passing the ATC ramp of the Shrivenham distant. Cozens glanced up from his firing and observed the signal itself showing clear. He piled on another couple of shovelfuls and looked up again and saw to his consternation three red lights apparently rushing towards them. Driver Starr had simultaneously seen the same terrifying phenomenon and immediately shut off steam and applied the brake, but their speed was only slightly checked before the lights were upon them. Actually it was they who were upon the lights, for it was only an illusion that made them appear to be moving. They were in fact the red lights (one tail and two side) on the rear of a stationary six-wheeled brake van belonging to a coal train. The van and five wagons had been left behind when a drawhook had broken, leaving them marooned in the middle of nowhere. The 474-ton express ploughed into the van and the latter's frame took much of the force of the collision, but as it collapsed so did the three coal wagons behind it and their wheels piled up. The other two wagons were propelled 1½ miles up the line with the enormous shock of the impact. The 4–6–0 King rode up on the heap of wagon wheels and turned over on its right side with its boiler along the down line.

The leading coach of the express, a corridor-third, detached itself at both ends and was thrown clear of the train sideways. The heavy steel frame ended up on the other track, but the wooden body with its steel panels carried on further and rolled down the slight embankment onto its roof. Extraordinarily the front half of the carriage was sufficiently undamaged that the doors could still be opened, while the rear five compartments were destroyed. There were about thirty-four passengers in the coach and, not surprisingly, most of the ten seriously injured in the crash were found here, as was the body of a woman – the only passenger fatality. The second vehicle was an older all-wooden bodied newspaper and guard's van and this was completely wrecked but luckily there was no one in it.

It was exceptional for such a van not to be the leading coach but on this occasion a carriage from the Torquay branch had been added to the front of the train at Newton Abbot while the engine was being changed. It was this coach that now lay half-shattered and upside-down with its stricken occupants. Whether or not the impact on this carriage would have been lessened if it had been marshalled behind instead of in front of the van is a matter for conjecture, but it is perhaps significant that the Company decided afterwards that in future a brake van would always be the leading vehicle on all its long-distance trains if at all possible.

The third coach was the first of four sleeping cars. It had a massive steel underframe and the body and roof were entirely encased in steel plating. It was derailed but stayed upright and in line and was not seriously damaged. In fact the remainder of the train was little affected considering the force of the crash. Indeed the fourth vehicle, another sleeper, was the only other coach to even leave the rails.

The locomotive, however, was severely damaged and the fireman was very fortunate to escape. Luck was not with Driver Starr, though, and he was trapped in the wreckage. It took hours to release him and he died from his injuries. A dramatic image is created by a contemporary newspaper report which claimed that when they finally reached the dying man his hand was still on the brake. He was the only other person killed by the accident.

So how had it happened? How had the signals come to have been cleared for the express when part of the preceding train was still in the section? The ATC had done its job and could not help in these circumstances, but what of the track circuit? Why had that not revealed the presence of the goods wagons and guard's van? For the answers we must go back about twenty-five minutes and about 4½ miles – back, in fact, down the line to the junction with the old Highworth branch. Here at 5 am the loaded coal train was running some three hours late after being delayed at Swindon, and was now making its laborious way forward towards its destination at Old Oak Common.

Driver D. G. Davis and his fireman, P. T. G. Jenkins, their names betraying the train's Welsh origin, were on the footplate of a 2–8–0 engine, no. 2802, and were getting the speed up gradually after the long interruption to their journey. A couple of minutes later at Marston Crossing

23. Shrivenham, 1936. Railway officials and a local policeman survey the devastated locomotive, 'King William III', its chimney lying pathetically detached on the lineside. On the left is the body of the leading coach, which was added so unwisely at Newton Abbot, its forward part still mostly intact. Its frame was left up on the track behind the tender on the down line. Note the persisting heavy frost – as on the grass and fence posts in the left-hand foreground – even though this photograph was obviously taken very much later in the day.

box they were doing about 20 mph. Davis looked back along the train and observed the right-hand side light of the guard's van, something he had done many times during the run as required by the rules. Davis knew the road well and recognised the Shrivenham distant signal and saw that it was clear. Ashbury Crossing distant, however, was at warning to prepare for the crossover to the goods loop. Access to the loop could, of course, also be gained by going through the up platform line but the normal and authorised procedure was to cross freight trains by the junction provided a little further on. Davis closed the regulator and reduced speed to negotiate the points. The train then entered the loop and continued on to Knighton Crossing where it came to a stand at the home signal to wait for the express to go by before rejoining the main line.

Davis and Jenkins had felt nothing untoward all this time. However, neither had looked back since Marston to check the side lights of the end of their train. Had they done so it's true that they might at first have thought that the intermittent mist that had built up around them was obscuring their view – the train was, after all, some 350 yards long – but when they had entered the loop it would have been a particularly good and relevant time to check that the whole train had successfully followed them. Davis told the inquiry that it was not 'customary' to do so at this point, so they had not.

The guard's van was in the charge of H. E. Chandler of the spare link at Severn Tunnel Junction. He was much less familiar with the line and had not worked a train over it for four months. After leaving Swindon he had occupied himself with paperwork and also spent some time working out what train he might get back from Didcot if, as he hoped, he was relieved there. He didn't notice Marston Crossing box but in his statement he said that he soon became aware that they were slowing down and after about seven minutes or so, at 5.20 by his watch, they had come to a standstill so he put his brake on very slightly. He continued:

I personally was of the definite opinion that the whole of the train was intact, and that we had come to a stand at Shrivenham home signal.

After coming to a stand, I looked through the end window of my van and sighted the Shrivenham signal box. I went through my van onto the verandah which was at the trailing end, and looked along the train with a view to seeing whether my train was intact and whether we were in fact at the home signal. It was then that I realised that my train had parted and that I only had the brake van and five wagons . . .

A glance to the rear a fraction later showed to my horror an express approaching on me. I gathered my flags and detonators, and, waving a red hand lamp violently, I raced to the rear, but I had not time to place down detonators . . .

I should say the express was about a mile or a mile and a half away when I first saw it. It is a perfectly straight road and I could see the headlights of the engine. I immediately raced back on the 6-foot side of the down main line and should say I ran back about 75 yards, but I am not quite sure of the distance.

Back along the line, 2 miles from Shrivenham station, lay part of a broken wrought-iron drawhook from the rear of a 12-ton goods wagon – the forty-eighth of the fifty-three of which the train was composed. No sudden jolt or extra strain had caused the hook's failure, just metal fatigue due to a combination of overheating during the casting process and the effect on that intrinsic weakness of the very low ambient temperature here. Drawhook failures were by no means uncommon – there had been more than 3,000 in the previous year in trains en route, and that typical figure took no account of the much larger number of fractures that occurred during shunting. There were higher standards already established for the requisite tensile strength of such gear for newly fitted hooks and bars, which were now only to be made of steel, but existing wrought-iron equipment did not have to be withdrawn.

Failures, then, were common, but accidents arising from them were not – for the simple and obvious reason that safety procedures existed to *see* that they were not. This breakage should have led to no more than an irritating delay to the oncoming passenger train. So although the fracture was the catalyst it was not the cause.

The guard said that he had had no time to protect the rear of his detached segment of the train before the express was upon it. But what of the signalmen? How had they failed to prevent the disaster? The train had been intact when it passed Marston Crossing box and the fact was duly noted by the man on duty there who recorded it in his register. The next box was Shrivenham.

Signalman W. Head had worked in Shrivenham box for seventeen years. His shift on this day began at 10 pm the previous evening but he was not unduly tired having slept well beforehand. As the coal train passed his box there was a down train of milk empties also going by and Head stayed at the Swindon end to see its single tail light before turning to look for the three lamps on the back of the up train as he walked along to put the down signals to danger. In his twenty-five years as a signalman he had never had an incomplete train pass his box, and he was sure this time too that he saw what he had expected to see. There was the slight mist, of course, and some remaining steam from the

down train, but he swore that he saw a tail lamp – only one, but that was enough – as the train passed the goods shed. Three minutes later he was asked 'Line Clear?' for the express from Marston Crossing and he gave the affirmative unhesitatingly.

Four minutes after that he accepted 'Train On Line'. A minute later he heard a bang and the up distant signal-lever shook violently. His first thought was that the train might have hit a cow on the line and he ran to the window but could neither see nor hear anything more. To be on the safe side he rushed over and threw his down signals to danger having cleared them for an empty stock train that had already passed the home signal. It was some measure of redemption since it prevented the train rushing headlong into the wreckage. The footplatemen on the empty stock train were keeping a good lookout and saw just in time that Head had reversed his starter to danger. They pulled up alongside the box and later went on to give valuable help at the accident when it became clear what had happened.

So often in other accidents have railmen managed to mis-see something or see what they expected to see even if, for once, it wasn't there. But on this occasion it would have taken more than Head's self-delusion about the tail lights to cause the crash. The man in the next box up would also have had to make a comparable mistake or wrong assumption. The odds were very much against such a coincidence – but evil chance was abroad and that is exactly what happened.

Signalman E. J. Jefferies, in Ashbury Crossing box, had only one train to deal with at the relevant time, but just as it had started to pass the box he said that the phone had rung and he had gone to the back of the box to answer it. It was Swindon advising him of a later train and by the time he had finished the call, and gone

24. Shrivenham, 1936. The leading coach seen from the other side – with the inevitable crowd of gawping sightseers beyond. The doors of the front compartments were easily opened and that half little damaged, while the total wreck of the rear five compartments can be seen to the right of the policeman at the top of the embankment. The roof in the foreground is from the newspaper-cum-guard's van that was marshalled second. The state of the Torquay coach illustrates well how little separated the two kinds of fate for passengers in these wooden-bodied carriages. Even those fitted with steel panels, like this one, offered little protection under major impact and barely survived lesser ones. Today's rolling stock, with its all-steel construction and vastly superior design, would have withstood this kind of crash little damaged – as has been shown in more than one incident in recent years.

back to the London-end window, the train had passed. He was sure, he said, that he saw a white light up the loop – which would have been correct as the guard would have changed a side light from red to white on entering the loop. Also, as was his practice, he looked along the line towards Shrivenham before sending 'Train Out Of Section'. Naturally he saw nothing unusual there. Had he seen that the train was incomplete, and he had warned Head straightaway, there would still have been time to stop the express before it reached the wagons which were then just coasting to a standstill on the other side of Shrivenham.

Jefferies was a man with nineteen years' service and had been at Ashbury Crossing for nine of them. So here were two highly experienced signalmen with good records and well used to their boxes. Yet in that icy-cold, dark, misty morning they both saw something, so they swore, that simply wasn't there.

Lt-Col A. H. L. Mount presided over the inquiry, as he had over many others, and his task was made initially more difficult by the fact that nearly all the clocks and watches involved in the incident appeared to have been telling different times! Since there were discrepancies between some of the key statements and time was a crucial factor, it was essential to establish, as far as possible, the real time at which all the contributing events occurred. Synchronisation of signal box clocks was improved as a result of this aspect of the matter. Having sorted out the times as best he could, the Inspector was able to weigh the statements with some degree of accuracy and found more than one of them wanting.

The guard of the coal train, Chandler, had obviously not given an accurate account of events. Further he had failed to obey Rule 148(b), which required him to keep a good look-out, and Rule 148(d) which would have caused him to make full use of his brake if he had thought the train was being stopped on this falling gradient. He had suggested that when his van had finally come to a standstill he saw the lights of the express only a mile or so away, but this was not possible as the express did not even enter the section until a full minute after that and would have been all of 2 miles away at that time. Lt-Col Mount concluded that the situation dawned on him only in time for him to leap out and save his own life. He had had, at the very least, six minutes to take preventive action and, even after his van had stopped, could have protected the rear of the train and reduced the severity of the collision by giving Driver Starr some effective warning. The Inspector attached a considerable amount of blame to Chandler. It was a tragic disgrace for a man who had not only a good record as a railwayman but had served with honour in the Great War where he had suffered gassing and had been a prisoner of the Germans.

Chandler was not held primarily responsible, however. That terrible distinction was shared by signalmen Head and Jefferies. Head had not pleaded any extenuating circumstances and it could only be put down to a simple, though serious, lapse on his part that he failed to observe the absence of tail lights. It was to his credit, though, that he had reacted so quickly on sensing the possibility that disaster had struck and thus prevented it from becoming very much worse.

Jefferies shared the blame equally as he too had failed in the basic duty to observe the tail lights. Unlike Head, he had had only one train to watch at the time so his omission was all the more inexcusable. Lt-Col Mount also made it clear that he doubted that a telephone call from Swindon had come at the time Jefferies claimed, since available evidence did not support this and he could not identify the caller. Without the opportunity to take any ameliorating action after his mistake, Jefferies came out of the investigation the most blackened.

The Inspector must have had a sense of déjà vu during this inquiry because the whole affair was strikingly similar to an accident that he had investigated in 1931. Near Dagenham Dock, on the LMS line from Fenchurch Street to Southend, a passenger train had run into the guard's van and ten wagons marooned by a freight train when a drawbar had broken. The guard had been less fortunate than Chandler as he had not even been aware of the separation when the locomotive smashed into his van and killed him, but his mistake was the same. There were no fewer than three signalmen involved and, like Head and Jefferies, they had failed to check the tail lights correctly and were all held to have been negligent.

The record in this respect, however, was not set until 1955 when on 20 January a Leicester–Manchester train collided with a divided freight train at Weekday Cross in Nottingham. It happened in early morning fog and the train was going very slowly so the effects were not serious, but the startling feature of the incident was that the incomplete front part of the goods train had passed *six* signal boxes in that condition and *none* of the signalmen had observed the fact!

Between the times of the Dagenham Dock and Shrivenham accidents there had been some improvement in the reliability of drawgear, but it was still a cause for concern on freight trains not fitted with continuous brakes. Lt-Col Mount detailed some further measures that he would like to see taken in this respect and repeated his Dagenham recommendation that wagons with obsolete types of casting should have them replaced at their next seven-year overhaul. Had this practice been adopted when he had first suggested it then the drawhook that had broken at Shrivenham would have been scrapped in 1932 and the accident would not have happened.

But it was the failure to observe the block regulations properly that had, as at Dagenham, led to the dreadful results of the breakaway. The accident, he said, was not the outcome of forgetfulness, incapacity or overwork but of plain failure on the part of the two signalmen, together with a lack of zeal and alertness on the part of the guard. The coal train's footplate crew could have prevented it if they had done at Ashbury what they had done at Marston, but they were under no specific obligation to do so at this point. A review of the regulation concerning the checking of tail lights by drivers and firemen was therefore thought to be desirable.

GWR was commended on its method of coach construction which had obviously been responsible for the comparatively low casualty list, though the Lieutenant-Colonel obviously felt that they might have been unwise to abandon buck-eye couplings which had kept coaches upright and in line in other accidents and are standard today. The Great Western had experimented with them from 1922 to 1929 but had decided to remove them all by 1931. The initial cost, plus the problems of carriages so fitted being used amongst conventionally equipped stock during the transitional period, did not seem to be outweighed by the advantages on the relatively safe GWR.

And what of the safety equipment installed at Shrivenham? The ATC may not have been relevant, but what of the track circuits? Well, these ran for 500 yards up to the home signals. The breakaway wagons stopped between the distant signal and the start of the up circuit and so were undetected by it. Track circuiting throughout the block section would have betrayed their presence, of course, and this was the ideal arrangement. Indeed at Oakham in Rutland (on the LMS line from Melton Mowbray to Kettering) only the previous year, a similar though less serious collision between a goods train and thirty-nine stationary wagons, left behind by a preceding freight train after the failure of a three-link coupling, would have been averted by such continuous track circuiting. The accident at Welwyn Garden City, as we have seen, would also have been averted by that means as would another at King's Langley in the same year. Four within a twelvemonth. However, with so many places still lacking the more basic circuits like those at Shrivenham, the urgency was to extend the use of home signal ones first. Of the sixty-five accidents of all kinds on the railways of Britain which were the subject of inquiries in the five years up to the end of 1934, no less than fourteen would have been prevented with these simple track circuits.

Indeed, unlike this foursome, none would have been more effectively prevented with a fully comprehensive one.

It was more of the ill luck pervading the desolate landscape on that winter Wednesday at Shrivenham that caused the wagons to stop just 180 yards short of the circuit. They had rolled down the 1 in 834 gradient for a full 1¼ miles from the time that the drawhook had broken; had the train's speed been a fraction greater at that moment they would have coasted those crucial few yards further, the track circuit would have shorted and Head would have had sufficient warning to stop the express. As it was, nothing led him to reconsider his fatal assumption that the whole goods train had gone by – nothing, that is, until the frenzied quivering of the signal-lever, and then it was too late. But on such chance fractions do lives so often depend.

The Shrivenham crash heralded the end of fifty years of immunity from major disaster on the Great Western. As mentioned in *Trains to Nowhere*, from Norton Fitzwarren in 1890 to, ironically, Norton Fitzwarren again in 1940, there was no accident with a high casualty list on the Company's lines. Much of this record was due to the policy of installing safety devices of proven merit like track circuits and the ATC that the Great Western had itself developed from 1906.

The human factor always finds ways, albeit quite unintentionally, to undermine the most carefully planned safety systems. Apparently unimportant rules are inclined to be overlooked and others 'adapted' to easier working. In most cases it makes no difference to the end result because nothing ever goes seriously wrong; but now and then on an ill-starred day, like that one at Shrivenham, several bent rules compound into tragedy. That day was a sad tale of failure: failure of equipment initially, but even more, and ultimately, the failure of men. Not stupid or irresponsible or even inexperienced men, but ordinary, decent, hardworking men who, on this one vital occasion, were tested and found wanting. Once again we are forced to the conclusion that, come what may, human beings it would seem insist on being 'only human'.

Shrivenham, like Norton Fitzwarren, belongs to that list of ill-fated places that appear more than once in the records of railway disasters. The coincidence here, though, was of a most exceptional kind since the earlier incident also involved an express which collided with stray wagons. Nearly 100 years before 'King William III' ran into the back of that guard's van, on 10 May 1848 to be precise, one of its broad gauge ancestors, on an up express from Exeter, ran into a cattle van and a horsebox that had been pushed out onto the main line to clear a turntable. Six died and thirteen were injured in what turned out to be the only really serious accident ever to befall a Great Western broad gauge express. Even in this circumstance the seven-foot width proved its worth when it came to stability, for the Daniel Gooch locomotive 'Sultan', with its 8-foot diameter single driving wheels, held the rails as did the whole train. The principal damage to the train occurred because the obstructing wagons, which had been hurled onto the station platforms, fell back onto the carriages as they raced by. There were, of course, far fewer safeguards then to prevent such a thing happening. Who would have thought that a century later it would still be possible for such a similar accident to occur – and at the same place. Progress can seem painfully slow at times.

10
Braysdown and Bath
(Somerset & Dorset Joint Railway)

The vast majority of railway accidents are, and always have been, trivial in nature and merit at most a few lines in the local press – or on the apology boards at affected stations! They are usually minor derailments of slow-moving vehicles and involve no significant injuries. Inevitably the casualty toll tends to rise in size and seriousness roughly in proportion to the scale of the accident. It is rare to find a mishap of consequence that is free from the physical distress of those involved, but the events at Braysdown on 29 July 1936 were of that exceptional nature. They even had about them an element of farce that would not have been out of place in a silent film comedy.

Braysdown is a tiny locality which lies between Radstock and Wellow in the new county of Avon. This little rural backwater belongs to the sad list of places that have seen the metals come and go, but in the 'thirties it was quite a busy railway site. In those days it belonged to Somerset and was on the line running from Evercreech Junction to Bath on the Somerset & Dorset Joint Railway. It did not merit a station but gave its name to a signal box and a colliery. The box was concerned with the sidings at the

colliery and also those at Writhlington Colliery nearby, as well as the double-track through line.

The original cabin on the site – actually some 50 yards to the north – was built in 1875 and named after the nearest significant feature on the landscape at the time: the hamlet of Foxcote about a mile away. It had stood for only a year when it was witness to the worst accident ever to occur on the S&DJR. The line between Radstock and Wellow was then only single track. On 7 August 1876, being a Bank Holiday Monday, there were a large number of extra trains being run and two of them collided head-on. The crash, which killed twelve passengers and one of the guards, brought to light a scandalous state of affairs in which ill-supervised, inexperienced, barely literate and appallingly overworked teenagers were being left, late in the evenings, to control the traffic. A telegraph and crossing-order system was in use at the time – a system that had already led to other serious head-on collisions elsewhere – and the 15-year-old who had been left in charge of Wellow station forgot to telegraph notice of one of the trains to his 16-year-old colleague in Foxcote box. The affair led to a major revolution in operating procedures.

With the doubling of the line and new sidings needed for the developing coalfield, Foxcote box was demolished and resited. The opportunity was taken to give the new signal box a now more appropriate name and Braysdown was chosen in honour of the adjacent colliery connected by a tramway from sidings opposite the box. Later it was to become Braysdown & Writhlington and, finally, just Writhlington after the closure of the other colliery. The long arm of coincidence, however, found the place despite the original change of name – though it did take it nearly ninety years. This time, though, the results were far from tragic.

To the north of the box there was a trailing crossover between the running lines, and trailing points in the up (Bath-bound) line leading onto Braysdown Colliery sidings on the west. There was a similar arrangement to the south of the box where the trailing points were in the down line and gave access to Writhlington

Colliery on the east side. The diagram makes clear the essentials.

It was a fine, clear summer morning at about 9.10 when no. 7620, a 3F 0–6–0 tank engine, came bunker-first along the up line from Radstock with a train of empty wagons to exchange for full ones from the two collieries. This daily procedure involved much shunting between the sidings via the crossovers and this Wednesday morning was no exception. No. 7620 had been bustling about for nearly half an hour when it manoeuvred eight empty wagons onto the up line a few yards north of the Braysdown Colliery points and left them there whilst it went off into the Writhlington Colliery sidings.

Signalman Haines in the nearby box was about to send the 'Blocking Back' signal, somewhat belatedly, to Radstock East in respect of these wagons when the phone rang. It was the Control Office to instruct him to shunt onto the down line an up freight train that was shortly due and thus allow a following passenger train to overtake it. When he put the phone down he began to plan the movements that would be

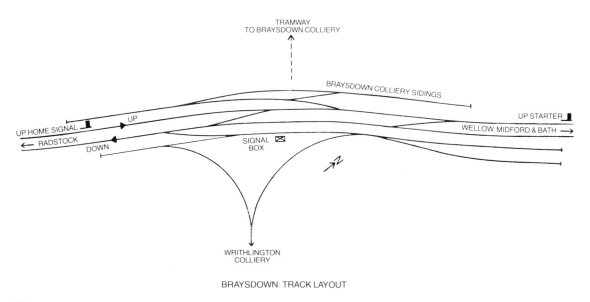

BRAYSDOWN: TRACK LAYOUT

78

Some idea of the terrific crash at Midford can be gauged from this picture of the wrecked signal box.

The scene in the gardens of Lynwood, Midford, near Bath, showing how the goods trucks came to rest after running away down the line. In the picture are Mr W. H. Berry, a visitor to the house, and Mrs Sayer, who had miraculous escapes.

By permission of the British Library

25. Braysdown. How the local paper showed the effect of the runaway on little Midford. The signal box was on the point of total collapse after the destruction of most of its base, whilst in the second picture can be seen just how close was the householders' escape, judging by the proximity of the coal wagon in the foreground to the corner of the building just visible on the left. At the top of the steep embankment down which the trucks tumbled can be glimpsed the valanced awning of the station platform.

necessary to comply with the instruction and forgot that he had not blocked back.

It was now 9.50 am and Haines accepted the freight train from Radstock East but of course did not clear any of his signals for it. He decided to get the wagons pushed further up the line so that he could let the train go forward clear of the southern crossover and thus set back onto the down line. He would then clear the wagons out of the way of the passenger train. No. 7620 was by now down in Writhlington Colliery sidings and Haines had to get hold of the shunter, Ash, to arrange for all this to proceed. Points moved this way and that and the engine went back over to the wagons.

'Train Entering Section' sounded in the box and almost immediately afterwards Haines was horrified to see the freight train over-running the home signal despite the fact that it was firmly and obviously at danger.

The freight train was the 8.10 am from Evercreech Junction which ran only as required and on this morning consisted of thirty-seven wagons and a brake van. It was headed by a 7F S&D Joint Railway built 2–8–0 engine, no. 13803, running chimney-first. The driver, Brewer, had been qualified for only three years but had been familiar with the line for much longer than that, having worked over it for

79

26. Braysdown. Midford Viaduct seen in August 1982. A view taken from the site of the signal box looking towards Wellow and Braysdown. Not just undergrowth but trees grow now where the escaped engine raced across propelling the rattling wagons.

Malcolm Gerard

many years as a fireman. He was, in fact, not a fully fledged driver even then, being classed, like Bell at Darlington, as a 'Passed Fireman', but he had acted as a driver more than a hundred times. His fireman, Hiroms, was new to him and very much his junior. Indeed, when Brewer had started working with the Company nineteen years previously, Hiroms was a newly born infant. Although he had done nearly a couple of hundred firing turns, most of these had been on shunting duties around Birmingham. Brewer was therefore none too sure of his ability and was watching him closely. Being still as much of a fireman as a driver himself, he was especially critical of the way the lad was doing the job and had been giving him some advice on breaking up clinker in the fire. He was supervising this operation when they approached the Braysdown distant signal and so failed to see that it was 'on'.

They were doing about 20 mph and, having no idea that they were going to be set back onto the down line, were not anticipating a stop. There was a climb ahead, from Midford up to Combe Down tunnel, which included a stretch of 1 in 50 gradient, and Brewer was anxious to see that the fire was well prepared for this. He told Hiroms to put on a few more shovels of coal and, watching him do this, almost missed seeing the home signal too. He glanced up just in time and grabbed the steam brake which he applied fully. He looked ahead and saw no. 7620 facing him. It is not hard to imagine his consternation! It looked as if a head-on collision was imminent. He quickly threw the engine into reverse and opened the regulator, but he had failed to secure the handle of the screw reversing gear in the back position and it spun round putting the engine into forward gear again. He then tried to close the regulator but it seemed to jam slightly open. He looked out again but there was steam coming from a leaky gland and he could not make out whether or not no. 7620 was in motion, let alone which way it was going. Feel-

80

ing that a collision was inevitable, and fearing that it might be severe, he panicked and shouted to his young fireman to jump. Hiroms needed no second prompting and Brewer followed him close behind.

The tank engine still had 10 yards to back up towards the wagons before Ash could couple them when the shunter saw the freight train approaching less than 40 yards away. He shouted to Driver Rawlings on no. 7620 who, on hearing him, turned round and saw the oncoming train for himself. He opened the regulator fully to lessen the impact and he and his fireman, Parker, jumped off just as their engine contacted the wagons towards which it had been moving.

Once on the ground, Rawlings realised that the advancing 2–8–0 was only doing about 5 mph, the engine brake that Brewer had applied having largely overcome the effect of the partially open regulator. Seeing its crew also on the ground, applying wagon brakes to increase the drag, he jumped up onto the footplate where he found no difficulty in closing the regulator fully. The train came to a standstill with the engines confronting each other close to the starting signal. Who could blame him if he felt a surge of pride and self-satisfaction at that moment? Had he not averted a collision? In this case pride, as so often happens, was simply the forerunner of a fall. Even as he felt the train clank to a stop, no. 7620, having merely been kissed gently on the buffers by the 2–8–0, was puffing away merrily propelling the eight wagons up the line behind its bunker.

Signalman Haines, seeing the locomotive steaming off round the bend, sent 'Train Running Away On Right Line' to the next box, Wellow. He had not seen clearly what had been happening and had no reason to suspect the unlikely fact that it was unattended. It wasn't until Ash came running up and told him the extent of

the drama that he phoned ahead to warn Signalman Banfield at Wellow. He also tried unsuccessfully to contact the Control Office at Bath.

The runaway had got up a good speed by the time it had covered the 3 miles down the gently falling gradient to Wellow, and rushed past the helpless signalman there at about 50 mph with the wagons still rattling along in front. On and on it went, along the constantly curving and undulating line towards Midford which was about 2½ miles further on. Here the twin tracks converged and became a single one. The points for this were just south of the station on the 150-yard long brick viaduct which crosses the B3110, a stream, and the old GWR Camerton branch – itself on a smaller viaduct. Midford signal box was between the viaduct and the station at the end of the platform. Both the box and the station were on the west of the line which was cut into the side of a hill at this point. The ground falls steeply opposite the platform and the line had to be supported by a 40-foot high retaining wall for about 60 yards north of the viaduct.

Signalman Larcombe had the points set and bolted for the down line and all was tranquil in this pleasant rural location when suddenly the peace was broken by the 'Train Running Away . . .' bell code from Wellow. Larcombe had begun the regulation procedures when it was followed up with a phone call from Signalman Banfield to warn him that there was no one on board the unorthodox train that would shortly be with him. He called the stationmaster and had only just time to tell him the gist of it when no. 7620 came into sight on the other side of the viaduct. With the help of the falling gradient, it had taken only three minutes to cover the distance between the two boxes and its vanguard of wagons raced onto the masonry arches at close to 60 mph.

Larcombe did not change the points to favour

the fugitive since he had had no time to ensure that the line was clear ahead and there had been shunting going on at a private siding a little way up. He watched in horrified astonishment as the leading wagon struck the points, left the rails and careered towards him. It smashed into the brickwork base beneath him, displacing the locking frame and connections. The truck shattered and bits of it were distributed over a length of more than 90 yards.

Banfield, in the Wellow box, was at that moment trying to ring Bath Control Office but the demolition had severed the telephone connection and the receiver went dead in his hand. Bath was eventually informed four minutes later by Post Office telephone from Midford. Larcombe was very fortunate to escape injury as his cabin was bombarded with disintegrating wagon. Most of it ricocheted off the brickwork and littered the track with debris. The next six vehicles negotiated the points, sufficiently forced open by their preceding fellow, but came to grief on the wreckage littering the line. They were each in turn deflected down the embankment opposite the platform as they went through the station. On their way they damaged the retaining wall and demolished a couple of telegraph poles, and it was only the intervention of a signal post that diverted two of the wagons from crashing into a nearby house. The station buildings and platform were, however, less fortunate and did suffer some damage. Most important though was the continuing lack of casualties.

All this havoc had, not surprisingly, distorted the track, but the engine somehow kept the rails and pushed through it all using the remaining wagon as a kind of battering-ram. It served the purpose but began to break up once the station had been passed and by the time no. 7620 was ¼ mile north of Midford it was pushing less than half a truck with only one pair of wheels.

It was all that was left of the eight that had set off from Braysdown less than ten minutes before.

The strange duo travelled on up the incline, past the siding where shunting had mercifully just finished, to Combe Down tunnel and on up through its mile length, to emerge successfully and start the descent to Bath Junction. Having lost some speed up the hill they were accelerating again now the incline was again in their favour. On and ever onwards they went, through another tunnel, the ¼-mile long Devonshire, and on nearly another mile to the bridge under the meeting of Claude Avenue and Bridge Road at South Twerton on the southern outskirts of Bath.

Here it was that the end door of the ruined wagon became jammed under the engine's wheels and the truant tank loco left the track. It suffered little damage, however, although the water level had fallen below the firebox crown and it was a bit bent in places. Had it travelled just ¼ mile further it would have reached the junction and been diverted into a goods yard where they were ready to deal with it. It had, nonetheless, covered more than 8 miles on its crazy journey through the hills and dales of this picturesque route before coming to rest lying exhausted against the green pillow of the embankment under the Claude Avenue bridge.

I have based my telling of this tale on the facts as known and the probabilities as established by the Ministry of Transport's Inspector. As regards the events at Braysdown that preceded the runaway, there were essential discrepancies between the accounts of the several railwaymen involved. Lt-Col Woodhouse, summing up his inquiry, considered Signalman Haines' evidence to be somewhat less than accurate. He had claimed that the wagons had been much further up the line, by the starting signal in fact, when he had sent no. 7620 back to push them a little further still to comply with his impression of the

27. Bath. A press photo taken shortly after no. 89 had crashed into the wooden office building seen on the right.

block clearance point. He had only been in charge of the box for eight weeks but the distances were plainly shown on the cabin diagram and his instructing signalman remembered dealing with the clearance points. Even if the wagons had not been quite at the required place, it did not merit sending no. 7620 over to move them up less than 20 yards, which is the distance Haines said that he thought they were short of the 440-yard over-run; certainly not with a train already approaching. Although supported by Ash as to the position of the wagons at the crucial time, the signalman's account was rejected in favour of that of the crew of the tank engine who had said that the wagons had been standing only a short distance to the north of the siding points.

The main cause of the incident was certainly the failure to follow the Company's block regulations, and the decision to return the shunting engine onto the up line, so Haines was therefore held most to blame. He'd been a signalman for only two years, having worked his way up from porter during the previous nine. He was, however, not alone in receiving the Inspector's censure. The behaviour of the driver of the freight train, Brewer, was held to be deplorable and to have contributed in no small measure to the accident.

Having missed the distant signal he should have been especially alert to see the home signal as soon as possible. Seeing it at the earliest point, 600 yards ahead, on this rising gradient he could easily have brought the train to a standstill by it. These mistakes were hard to defend, but quite indefensible was the abandonment of his engine when it neared the other one. Neither locomotive was moving fast and he was running chimney-first so was reasonably well protected if a collision did occur. He had obviously panicked and for that he was heavily criticised. Young Hiroms, his fireman, could hardly be blamed for following his driver's instruction to jump.

The crew of the other engine, the runaway itself, were considered both to be at fault. Lt-Col Woodhouse found it hard to believe Rawlings' assertion that he knew there was no one on board the approaching engine, since he admitted that he had not seen its crew on the ground until after he had left his own footplate. He claimed to have shouted to his fireman to take charge whilst he dealt with the oncoming train by applying wagon brakes. Parker, though, had no recollection of being so ordered. To leave his post with the regulator open, and no clear agreement with his mate that he was being left in charge, was deserving of severe stricture. Rawlings' subsequent action in taking control of the other engine did little to mitigate his behaviour since it was apparently not a matter requiring any great measure of courage or initiative and was evidently something of an afterthought.

Parker had also been far too quick to leave the cab whether or not he had been told to take the controls. The bulk of the locomotive was placed protectively between him and the oncoming train, which was moving pretty slowly by the time his attention was drawn to it by the shouts of the shunter. Whilst appreciating the alarm both Parker and Rawlings had understandably felt in seeing the freight train no more than 40 yards away and closing, the Inspector felt they had unjustifiably lost their heads and deserted their posts with no thought of the consequences.

In the circumstances there were few changes in operating procedures that the Inspector could suggest to avoid the remote chance of a recurrence. An engine running away unattended with the regulator wide open was an unlikely enough occurrence in the first place. However, it was not unprecedented and there was also the more possible eventuality of a train running away out of its crew's control or vehicles breaking away down a gradient. He suggested, therefore, that in future the rule should be to pass on the news from box to box as it was received and *before* trying to stop or divert the runaway – thus giving maximum warning ahead should such efforts fail. Larcombe at Midford might have had a chance to prevent the damaging derailment at the points if Banfield at Wellow had been under an obligation to warn him before assembling detonators and red flag as he had done on receipt of the bell code from Haines. The futility of such equipment, even if he had time to make use of it, not being apparent until the subsequent phone call from Braysdown.

The Lieutenant-Colonel, having had to do so much scolding, was at least able to record that, for once, there were no deaths or casualties of any animal kind. A few lineside items, a bit of permanent way and some rolling stock had suffered somewhat, and Midford station took a while to recover, but all in all the humour of the situation can be appreciated without any qualifying qualms about human suffering.

'The Pines Express' had to be diverted but traffic was back to normal by seven that evening. The ability of our railways to patch themselves up and carry on as quickly as possible has always been one of their most commendable

Illustrated London News

28. Bath. The next day, seen from the other side, with the wagon repairing company's sign ironically overlooking a mass of mutilated trucks beyond any hope of repair.

characteristics and has often been less than fully appreciated.

Coincidence, as we have seen before and shall see again, seems to haunt railway lines. It certainly haunted this stretch of the Somerset & Dorset, for the Braysdown runaway was something of a comic epilogue to a strangely similar (but much unhappier) drama that had taken place some seven years earlier.

Let us visit Signalman Larcombe again at Midford. Not on 29 July 1936 this time, but back on 20 November 1929. It was that day, also

a Wednesday, that Larcombe must himself have recalled when seeing no. 7620 rushing towards him. On that earlier occasion, at about six in the evening, he was the last person apart from his fireman to speak to the doomed driver of what was to become another runaway locomotive. The footplate was not empty that time, however.

It was dark and damp. Another of the big 7F 2–8–0 engines, no. 89, with a six-wheeled tender, specially built at Derby in 1925 for the steeply graded line, was pulling a 38-vehicle train laden mostly with coal. This engine was essentially the same as the one that Brewer had in his charge, and it too was running from Ever-creech to Bath. Braysdown was well past, though, and it had been stopped at Midford up outer home signal to wait for two down trains to go by. When the second had gone it was shunted over the viaduct and then set back onto the down line to allow a Bournemouth–Bath passenger train to overtake it – shades of the other incident again.

Driver Jennings took it 300 yards back along the down line so that he would have a good run at the steep gradient beyond the station. He left his fireman, Pearce, in charge and walked back over the viaduct to the signal box. He told Larcombe that his engine was not steaming well and with such a heavy train (nearly 500 tons) he wanted to get up as much speed as possible for the climb. To help facilitate this he asked if he could stay in the box until the overtaking train had gone through and he could have the tablet that would allow him to proceed along the single line to Bath. The tablet-catcher on the engine would not work coming from the down line and his fireman might have difficulty pick-ing it up in passing at the speed he hoped to be doing by that time. He might also have ventured the opinion that it would be preferable if up goods trains were shunted at Wellow for such predictable manoeuvres in view of the steepness of the gradient ahead.

They had been held up at Midford for more than an hour by the time the tablet was issued and Jennings and Pearce were able to get their train away. They got their speed up to 15 mph through the station but were down to about a quarter of that by the time they reached the tunnel that lay a mile or so further up. They were travelling tender-first and as they entered the single-track tunnel the atmosphere was noticeably thicker than usual and was very hot. The smoke from the three trains that had passed through it while they had been stuck at Midford, combined with that from their own heavily labouring one, made Pearce cough violently. Jennings was not obviously affected at first, as far as his fireman could see, but the fug soon became so bad that Pearce had to wrap his coat round his head to afford some measure of protection. It was not enough and he soon had to sit down as his head began to swim. A moment or two later he passed out.

Jennings must have tried desperately to fight against the effects of the poisonous, suffocating fumes and heat. But, somewhere during the ten minutes it took the toiling train to pass under Combe Down, he too succumbed. The regu-lator was between a quarter and one-third open and the machine was practically in full gear when he collapsed.

On finally crawling out of the tunnel the summit of the line had been reached and the speed picked up as the 1 in 50 down gradient had its effect. Faster and faster, through the short Devonshire tunnel and up to 50 or 60 mph. But the speed and the fresh air were not enough to revive either of the engine crew. The guard meanwhile, aware by now that all was not well, applied his brake harder and harder but to little avail.

The bottom of the gradient was only 100 yards before Bath Junction signal box and the line became double again there before joining the LMS metals another 100 yards beyond. The train dashed under the Claude Avenue bridge, round the long curve up over the Bristol Road and into the junction. It then clattered over the various points that had been set for it to run as scheduled into the Bath station yard.

The last of these points, designed for the slowest of shunting movements, finally de-feated the speeding engine and it left the rails, ran 50 yards along the ground between the tracks and smashed into the western end of the yard's office building. Being after office hours it was luckily nearly empty, but an inspector still on duty there was killed – as was a clerk making his way home across the yard. No. 89, in demolishing half the building, had discharged its enormous accumulated power and it came to a stop lying on its right side. The wagons piled up in a huge heap of wreckage leaving only the brake van upright, and indeed little damaged. The guard was no longer in it, having wisely jumped out before this point.

Rescue of the crew was hampered by the way the tender had overturned at an angle that blocked access to the footplate from either side. A gas pipe in the building had fractured and this, hazardously near to the engine's fire, combined with scalding steam, made the operation especially dangerous and difficult. It was not unlike dealing with an unexploded bomb in the blitz. Despite the risks there was no shortage of willing helpers, and both footplatemen were extracted alive. Jennings, however, lived only a few minutes before dying on his way to hospital.

Col A. C. Trench, in his remarks following the inquiry, noted that it was the first time in Combe Down tunnel's fifty years that footplatemen had been overcome by fumes, or even complained of more than a degree of discomfort consistent with other tunnels on gradients. This was quite surprising since it was the longest unventilated tunnel in the country and was notorious amongst drivers for its choking atmosphere. The Colonel concluded that it had been the high humidity and absence of wind in the prevailing weather which had combined on this occasion to hold most of the smoke from the previous trains. Add to this the presence of a poorly steaming engine dragging behind it a particularly heavy train, and you had a freak combination of factors unlikely to coincide again. But, remote though the chance was, Col Trench felt that precautions should be taken.

Better ventilation in the tunnel would be the ideal, of course, but if that were too costly to consider, then the use of banking engines or the reduction of loads should be contemplated.

He felt that working tender-first might not be desirable here as the cab of a loco tends to act as a cup and intensify the effect of any fumes – especially at slow speeds. There was no facility to turn engines of this class south of Bath on these journeys and a suitable turntable would obviously be a great asset. Ironically the first five of the 2–8–0s, built in 1914 by the Midland Railway Company at Derby, were fitted with tender cabs to allow for the frequent reverse working, but in 1921 these cabs were discontinued and the originals removed after complaints from their crews that they were inconvenient and uncomfortable.

Desirable though it might be to run chimney-first when possible, there was an advantage to be gained from running backwards in tunnels as the smoke from the engine itself tended to be left behind. This advantage increased with the speed being travelled and it was the low speed that had been the trouble in this case. The poisonous atmosphere of Combe Down tunnel on that distant November evening is an extreme but not wholly untypical example of the conditions often suffered by footplatemen in days gone by. The discomforts of smoke-filled tunnels and driving rain and snow are often forgotten when looking back through the warm unpolluted haze of nostalgia to the Great Days of Steam.

Thus both comedy and tragedy occurred on the Somerset & Dorset Joint Railway's much loved and much missed line. Even the collieries have closed and Braysdown has sunk back into the obscurity that places it beneath the recognition of most cartographers. The site of the old signal box can be found alongside the huge waste tip from the worked-out Writhlington Colliery on one of the most walkable stretches of the old line. But there is little there to enable one to recognise it. Wellow box has also gone, of course, but the station there has been lovingly converted into a private house, with a lawn between the platforms, and is still easily identified. Midford viaduct still stands, fenced off and overgrown on top. Where the signal box once stood there is now the car park of a neighbouring pub, but the platform still exists and can be walked along, pushing past the mass of weeds and wild flowers that thrive there. Combe Down and Devonshire tunnels are blocked up and still no doubt retain the smell of smoke that must permeate every crevice of the brickwork.

It was never a really viable line, but had it survived just a little while longer it might have reached the Great Age of Preservation which has saved at least part of many less appealing lines. What a shame that it did not.

I I
Soham
(London and North Eastern Railway)

In both world wars the railways were sorely tried in many ways. Not least amongst their problems was the disruption caused by enemy bombing. The danger from explosives was not, however, confined to those dropped by the Germans; there were grave risks involved in transporting armaments for our own side. The very high safety standards governing the carriage of ammunition and the like in peacetime had to be relaxed. In view of the enormous quantities of explosives carried in the last war, it is no mean achievement that comparatively little went off by accident. Fires in ammunition trains were the greatest hazard, usually caused by engine sparks, but even in that category there were only three fires in running trains which led to serious explosions in the years 1939 to 1945.

The most serious and certainly most dramatic of these did not happen until the weary penultimate year of the war. It happened in Cambridgeshire in the early hours of Friday 2 June 1944. A freight train from Whitemoor marshalling yard at March was taking a consignment of bombs and detonators to Ipswich. They had been manufactured in America and been landed at Immingham Docks near Grimsby. Their final destination, as far as the railway was concerned, was White Colne in Essex where they would be delivered to the United States Air Force.

The train was hauled by a wartime heavy goods 'Austerity' class 2–8–0, no. WD 7337, and was running chimney-first approaching Soham, on the LNER Ely–Newmarket branch, when Driver Ben Gimbert noticed flames coming from the leading SR wagon. Sulphur dust, left in the wagon after previous similar loads, and ignited by an engine spark getting under the covering sheet, would seem to have been the most likely cause. However it had started, the fire had got a good hold by the time it was apparent to the footplatemen. Gimbert, knowing that the wagon contained forty 500-lb bombs, decided to get it uncoupled and try and pull the truck through Soham and out into the open countryside before the inevitable explosion. In any event, he knew it must be separated from the rest of the highly volatile train.

He pulled up gently and came to a stand 90 yards short of the station. His fireman, Jim Nightall, hurried off to uncouple between the first and second wagons while Gimbert prepared to move off as quickly as possible. Nightall returned no more than a minute later having successfully accomplished his mission and the train moved off again smartly.

Reaching the platforms, Gimbert slowed to tell the signalman what he was doing and to ensure that he contacted the next box ahead to stop oncoming traffic. He knew that a mail train was due and, since the single line they had been on for the last 5 miles became double from this point, he was naturally anxious not to pass another train.

The fire was now burning very brightly and lit up the whole station: a blazing beacon in the blacked-out night. The signalman, Bridges, had come out of his box on the opposite platform to speak to the driver and was floodlit by the flames. He was just about to assure him that nothing had been accepted into the next section when the temperature of the roasting bombs reached the crucial level and 5 tons of high explosive unleashed its awesome destructive energy over the station and the sleeping little market town which lay alongside.

Fox Photos

29. Soham. Daylight revealed the full effect of the devastating explosion on this little Fenland town. The presence of so much helmeted military personnel adds to the impression of a battleground. The skeleton of the signal box on the down platform can be clearly seen on the right-hand side. Had Bridges not left his box to speak to Gimbert he would still have been very lucky not to have suffered a similar fate, although the stationmaster and his family survived the almost total destruction of the station house – the ruin in the centre of the picture.

In place of the wagon there was a crater 15 feet deep and 66 feet wide. It embraced both platforms to their full width and the only traces found of the vehicle were a buffer and socket casing. The rest was probably buried in the crater; there was no time to excavate it as the first priority was to restore traffic over this vital link as quickly as possible. The track was destroyed for a length of 40 yards. Much credit must be given to the railwaymen who had the task of repairing the damage for it was only just over eighteen hours later that the line was reopened.

The tender was transformed by the blast into a mass of twisted metal as it took the full force, but in doing so it substantially protected the engine which stayed upright, though derailed, and suffered no serious structural damage. However, the cab being at the most vulnerable end meant that it was the worst affected part and Jim Nightall was killed instantly. Ben Gimbert miraculously survived, though he had serious and extensive wounds and suffered, not surprisingly, from severe shock. The station was all but razed and Signalman Bridges died later in the day from the injuries he received. Five others were detained in hospital in serious condition, including the stationmaster who had been asleep in the station-house when it was demolished by the explosion. His family were amongst the twenty-two others who sustained lesser injuries.

Fifteen houses in the town were wrecked and three dozen more were rendered temporarily uninhabitable. Another 700 buildings were affected to some extent over a radius of about ½ mile. But just imagine how easily the devastation could have been multiplied many times if the engine's crew had decided to abandon their posts when the danger was recognised. By putting themselves in jeopardy they had prevented a chain reaction through the fifty other similarly loaded wagons that could virtu-ally have wiped Soham off the map. For even without the stop to uncouple they could not have cleared the town with their lethal load before the whole lot had gone up.

In the other two instances of such fires leading to major explosions in the last war, the foot-platemen managed to isolate the vehicles concerned in time to avoid results on the same scale – though in each case a driver died.

At Bootle (the one in Cumbria, not the one next to Liverpool in Merseyside) the driver of the train involved had not been told what was in the wagon that caught fire. He was killed when, having successfully separated it from the vehicles on either side, he went too close to the blazing truck. Fifty-two depth charges exploded on that occasion and again an engine spark was thought to have been responsible.

The Bootle incident was on 22 March 1945, and only a month later, on 18 April, the third of the tragic triad took place at Gascoigne Wood yard, near Selby in Yorkshire. This time the driver who was killed was on another engine nearby when some more 500-lb bombs exploded.

In all three cases the crews had acted bravely and efficiently, though only at Soham had there been a serious danger to a sizeable community. The risks to the driver and fireman there were the greatest too, and the inhabitants of that town were indeed fortunate that men of the calibre of Gimbert and Nightall were aboard that particular train on that terrible night.

In recognition of their selfless and courageous behaviour they were both awarded the George Cross – the highest award for civilian gallantry. For Nightall's family it was perhaps some compensation for their tragic loss.

Memories of heroic deeds are often short-lived, especially at a time when acts of comparable bravery were being performed daily across the Channel. However, the events of that

30. Soham. The 'Austerity' 2–8–0, no. WD 7337, being lifted from the debris of the disaster, showing the twisted cab in which Nightall died and his driver was seriously injured. The rest of the locomotive remains remarkably intact having suffered no serious damage, but little more than wheels can be identified of the tender.

Fox Photos

June night in Soham have transcended mere history and moved into the more enduring realms of legend. Only recently the heroism of the two men was recalled and marked by the naming of a couple of locomotives. At March station (Soham having closed in 1965), British Rail arranged a ceremony to christen two class 47 main line diesel-electric locos, nos 47577 and 47579. It was a fitting tribute. Hopefully 'Benjamin Gimbert GC' and 'James Nightall GC' will have many trouble-free miles to travel in their new guise.

12
Weedon and Blea Moor
(London Midland Region, BR)

During the development and operation of railways in Britain, sound engineering design and good maintenance have almost always been given high priority. In this century there have been very few serious accidents resulting from deficiencies in either. We come now to some of those exceptions; a group of inter-related events centring on two incidents that happened only six months apart and both on former LMS routes.

We visit first the parish of Weedon in Northamptonshire. The station there has gone now from the railway map, but the line through it is still very much a part of the system, being the electrified main line from Euston to Glasgow. In that disaster-laden year 1915, it had been the scene of a most unusual accident in which a coupling rod on a George V class 4–4–0 had come off its crankpin because the split-pin had fallen out and allowed the collar to unscrew itself. The train was safely brought to a stop, but not before the flailing rod had damaged the track in the path of a train going the opposite way. The double-headed down 'Irish Mail', running at 70 mph, had no warning of the danger and was immediately derailed – killing ten of those aboard and injuring sixty-four others.

A fitter had failed to open properly the ends of the split-pin. Having extorted such an obscenely high price for his carelessness, fate obviously decided that Weedon was a good location for such disasters – though waiting thirty-six years before striking there again. In 1951, on Friday 21 September, the 8.20 am up Liverpool–Euston express was running about a quarter of an hour late when it approached Weedon at around 11.15. It consisted of fifteen coaches headed by 4–6–2 class 8P Pacific no. 46207, 'Princess Arthur of Connaught' – based at Edge Hill, Liverpool. Doing something over 60 mph, it went into the 50-chain left-hand curve just beyond the station and the leading bogie wheels bounced up and over the rails to the right. This had no immediate effect discernible on the footplate and the train proceeded out of the curve and along the straight stretch following with its speed unchecked. However, ¾ mile further on, just beyond the short Stowe Hill tunnel, the flat-bottomed rails with shallow base-plates gave way to the older bull-head type. The Pacific's crew were still unaware that anything was

31. Weedon, 1951. The southern mouth of Stowe Hill tunnel gapes in the background at the wreck of the train it had so recently disgorged. The zigzag pattern of the coaches, so characteristic of accidents involving rapid deceleration, was a feature of both this crash and the one at Blea Moor. Here at Weedon the carriages have withstood the impact less well than did those at Blea Moor, but nonetheless it was principally due to improvements in coach construction that the casualty list was kept down to such a small percentage of those aboard. Note, just this side of the bridge, the buckled up road where the derailed bogie wheels began to smash against the chairs.

Popperfoto

wrong during the forty-five seconds or so that it took to cover the distance from the curve to the end of the tunnel. Then, as the new track gave way to the old, the derailed bogie wheels began to smash against the chairs and break up the track, sending the locomotive off to the left where it ran down the 12-foot embankment and fell onto its left-hand side. This being the driving side, the driver was buried in coal from the tender as it overturned, but he was not seriously hurt. The fireman escaped injury altogether.

Not so lucky were the occupants of the front coaches which were badly damaged. Seven passengers died outright, as did one of the dining car staff, and seven more died later in hospital. Many others were injured as all but the last two vehicles left the rails – piling up behind and alongside the engine and across both tracks. Such was the tremendous sound of the crash that it was clearly heard by the signalman in Heyford signal box over ½ mile ahead, and he was thus able to stop the approaching down 'Royal Scot' at his home signal and thus avoid a double disaster.

'Princess Arthur of Connaught' had been hauling its first train since a fortnightly routine 'X' examination the previous day. Ironically it was as a direct result of this examination that the accident occurred. It had been noticed that the left leading bogie wheel was wearing sharp and so the axles and their boxes were swopped round between the front and rear of the bogie. The fitter who carried out the job was an experienced man but he failed to ensure that the axle boxes had adequate freedom in the horns in which they were held. What was now the front axle box was too tight a fit and this stopped the wheels rising and falling properly under the action of the springs and so allow them to follow the normal variations of the track. It was perhaps surprising that they had held the rails for as long as they had – 130 miles. There must have been many another occasion that morning

32. Weedon, 1951. No. 46207, 'Princess Arthur of Connaught', where it ploughed into the field. It was lucky to find such an unobstructed escape route and such soft and welcoming earth to absorb its considerable momentum. The offending bogie looks innocently unaffected at a glance, but on closer inspection some damage is discernible to the rim of the leading wheel's flange.

when they had nearly jumped off. The curve at Weedon was comfortably within accepted tolerances of alignment so it was only chance that picked a spot so close to an earlier mis-adventure also caused by the uncharacteristic incompetence of a fitter.

The engine was not badly damaged by its upset, helped by the fact that it had come to rest in a field of soft earth, but was too far from the track for direct lift. A complicated plan was devised to haul it up the embankment and re-rail it with the minimum additional damage. A fort-night later the recovery was successfully accomplished.

The 1915 Weedon accident was one of another pair of incidents which were remark-ably similar. In both cases, because of lack of care with a split-pin, a connecting rod had come loose and damaged the opposite track and so involved another train. The other one of that pair was the 1960 accident at Settle, referred to in Chapter 4 and detailed in *Trains to Nowhere*. Mention of Settle takes us back to that dramatic line over the High Pennines where happened the third in a quartet of accidents attributable to locomotive defects and occurring within little more than a year of each other.

The second of the four had been at Glasgow Queen Street on 14 November 1951 and was due to a vacuum brake failure resulting from a long-standing defect that had remained through various maintenance checks. The light engine

involved had gone out of control whilst running tender-first on the steep gradient from Cowlairs and had collided with a rake of empty passenger coaches being manoeuvred over a scissors cross-ing at the entrance to the station. Seven railway staff were injured but, all things considered, it was a lucky escape. A hole had worn through the vacuum chamber flexible hosepipe between the engine and tender; also the outer air-valve spring of the vacuum ejector was found to be missing. There were signs that someone had tried to patch the hole at some time, but who and when was never established – not surprisingly no one came forward to admit it. The crash led to changes in the design and layout of such hoses to avoid rubbing in future.

The third part of the foursome of events re-ferred to was on 18 April 1952 at Blea Moor, near the Settle–Carlisle line's famous – and now crumbling – Ribblehead Viaduct.

It was another Friday and the 9.15 am 'Thames–Clyde Express' was on its way from Glasgow to St Pancras. The ten-coach train needed double-heading to get it smoothly up and over the 1,167 foot high Ais Gill summit The pilot locomotive was an old class 4P 4–4–0 compound, no. 41040, and behind it was a class 7P rebuilt Scot 4–6–0 no. 46117, 'Welsh Guardsman', as train engine. Having achieved the summit, the express made its way over the 10 miles of undulating terrain to Blea Moor tunnel – in which the 15-mile descent to Settle begins. Just before the tunnel, on the tender of the pilot engine, the front end of a brake rod came free and dropped down. It was the rod on the right-hand side and it immediately started bouncing on the ends of the sleepers. As happened with 'Princess Arthur of Connaught's' bogie wheels, the footplatemen were unaware that anything was amiss since the fault did not affect the ride. In both cases there would have been ample time to bring the trains to a safe

33 (*opposite*). Blea Moor. The leading coaches of the 'Thames–Clyde Express', with their bogies strewn all around, lie across the torn up track. The effect on the all-steel construction of the front three vehicles is in dramatic contrast to that on other rolling stock in many earlier accidents. That there should have been no fatalities in a well-loaded express in such a derailment is a remarkable tribute to all those who worked towards the introduction of such improved designs. Note the pilot engine, no. 41040, at the top of the picture, with only the rear of its offending tender off the rails; the blameless train engine lies on its side a few yards behind.

34. Blea Moor. The train engine, rebuilt Scot no. 46117, 'Welsh Guardsman', bearing its nostalgic headboard, lies in a bed of ballast after its encounter with the damaged points. Despite the sunshine, the bleakness of Blea Moor is apparent in the background.

Popperfoto

standstill had there been any hint that something untoward had occurred.

The 'Thames–Clyde Express' ran on through the 1½-mile long tunnel and out onto the aptly named Blea (short for Bleak) Moor. On this fine spring afternoon it may have somewhat belied its name, but in winter it is everything its title implies – a fact that the builders of the line discovered very early in the construction of this hard-won route. Blea Moor signal box, ¾ mile from the tunnel, was a comparatively new line-side feature, having been built as recently as the last war to control two new goods loops. The loose brake rod bounced along happily until it came to the facing points of the up loop where it struck the lock stretcher bar and forced open the closed switch rail – buckling itself badly in the process. The engine in front, having of course already cleared the points before this happened, was not much affected by this and remained upright, coming to a stop about 160 yards beyond the points with only the rear four wheels of the tender off the rails. The train engine, however, encountered the opened tongue of the damaged points and was straightaway overturned on its left-hand side onto the up loop line, coming to rest just behind the pilot.

The front four coaches were torn off their bogies and landed on their sides; the first three forming the all too familiar zigzag pattern across the tracks that is associated with accidents involving rapid deceleration and which was also a feature at Weedon a few months earlier. Most of the other carriages were derailed but kept in fairly good line. The leading coaches were badly damaged but they had steel underframes and the front three were new all-steel vehicles with buck-eye couplings and there was no telescoping. It was a major tribute to the advanced design of the rolling stock that there were no fatalities amongst the 200 people aboard despite the severity of the derailment. There were indeed only thirty-four injured and half of those did not have to be detained in hospital.

Actually getting the injured *to* hospital – in places as far apart as Skipton, Kendal, Leeds and Lancaster – was one of the principal problems faced by the rescue organisers. They were notified immediately, of course, by the signalman but there is no road near the site. A special train was dispatched as quickly as possible and sent down the line to take the casualties to Ribblehead station and thence by ambulances. A doctor who was on holiday in the area was contacted within minutes and he rushed for half an hour over the moor on foot to provide the first medical assistance.

The damage to the track was considerable, but once again we can observe that, as on so many other occasions, the permanent way staff did a magnificent job of rapid repairs and there was single-line working by the middle of the next morning with normal working resumed by the end of the afternoon.

Having cleared up the mess, the time had come to concentrate on the cause. Colonel D. McMullen conducted the official inquiry and established that the brake rod detachment was due to bad maintenance. The round pin holding the rod to the brake shaft had been displaced because the securing split-pin had dropped out. Like the 8P Pacific at Weedon the autumn before, the engine and tender had had an 'X' examination on the previous day. Although the fitters who had worked on the brake gear had not needed to remove the split-pin concerned, they should certainly have noticed its condition. Judging by the signs of wear on the round pin, found lying where the sleepers showed the first marks made by the brake rod, it must have been visibly in a poor state. Unlike the round pin, though, it could not be found – having no doubt fallen off many miles back. It was probable that one leg of the missing pin had sheared and it had dropped out because the other leg was not sufficiently splayed – or possibly had also sheared. The fitters claimed that the pins were all in order when they had worked on the tender, but Col McMullen was unable to accept this – especially as the equivalent split-pin on the other side was in far from good condition and he had examined the brake gear on a number of other engines and tenders at the same depot (Holbeck) and found other cases of ill-fitting split-pins with only one leg splayed. None were as bad as the opposite one on the tender involved in the derailment, but they were indicative of the fact that insufficient attention had obviously been given to brake gear there over a considerable period. In August 1944 there had been an almost identical accident on the LNER at Wood Green in North London – one of two serious derailments there in the same month – but the lessons of that incident had apparently still not been universally learnt.

After Blea Moor you would suppose that

special attention would have been given to split-pins on all locomotive brake gear at all Motive Power depots for a very long time afterwards. But as we have seen before, at St Bedes for instance, the experience expensively acquired by other railwaymen from other sheds on other Companies' lines (or on another region of the nationalised network as was to be the case now) is not necessarily taken advantage of elsewhere. Only six months later, on Saturday 25 October 1952, a strikingly similar accident occurred on the Southern. It completed the quartet of mishaps with the common factor of poor maintenance that had started such a little while before.

A Merchant Navy Pacific was hauling the eleven-coach 12.20 midday train from Ilfracombe to Waterloo. It was nearly 3.45 pm as it cleared Crewkerne and it was heading for Sutton Bingham at about 75 mph when the brake hanger on the rear of the left-hand trailing tender wheel detached itself and hung just clear of the sleepers. It remained in this position for nearly 3 miles, with, once again, the crew being unaware that there was anything wrong. Over this distance it struck glancing blows against check rails and fish bolts from time to time but not hard enough to unsettle the tender. Then the train reached an occupation crossing and the hanger caught in the throat of the check rail there and tore it off the track.

The check rail, which was nearly 11 feet long, rose up like a crude javelin aimed at the rest of the train and plunged diagonally through the floor and all four passenger compartments of the leading coach, emerging through the roof at the rear. This horrific event resulted, miraculously, in only one serious injury, though sadly that was a child. There were no deaths and only seven other passengers needed any kind of medical treatment. The train was, not surprisingly for such a run at that time of year, lightly loaded; it was indeed fortunate that it had not happened a

couple of months earlier when it would probably have had a full Saturday complement of returning holidaymakers.

The train ran on to Sutton Bingham station from where the injured were taken to hospital. Half an hour later, after temporary repairs to the engine, the train continued to Yeovil where the engine and damaged coach were removed.

The accident highlighted a design defect in the Merchant Navy class which had first been noticed after a similar, though much less serious incident at Woking in the previous December. Split-pins were again the crux of the matter – this time because of shearing that occurred due to there being no lubricating facility provided. The relevant pins rotated slightly every time the brakes were applied and the friction could eventually lead to the pins breaking in the middle – as had happened on these occasions. Inadequate examination in the workshops, hindered as it was by dirt in the relevant area, was a contributory factor, but essentially the design was at fault and modification followed.

Split-pins were, and still are, very hard things to replace satisfactorily in many areas of engineering. Properly used they are most effective and perfectly safe, but they are vulnerable to abuse and the carelessness of the less conscientious fitter. It would perhaps be more surprising if fewer accidents were attributable to defective split-pins in view of the countless ones used over the years.

Coincidence reared its head again when, in the following year, Crewkerne was once more the location for the breakdown of a Merchant Navy Pacific. No. 35020, 'Bibby Line', was heading an Exeter–Waterloo express at high speed when a crank axle failed. The train stopped safely and the cause was found to have been a creeping flaw under the chain sprocket of the valve gear which had not been unclamped from the axle since the locomotive had been

35. Crewkerne. Merchant Navy Pacific, no. 35020, 'Bibby Line', at Crewkerne on 24 April 1953 after the fracture of the driving axle.

W. S. Rendell and Son

built in 1945 – it not being part of routine maintenance that it should have been. As a result the Bulleid Pacifics were temporarily withdrawn from service for examination and the majority were found to have similar flaws, so new crank axles were fitted throughout.

The standard of locomotive design and maintenance had, by the second part of the twentieth century, reached a high and consistent standard – as the small number of serious defects bears witness. Improvements in coach construction and the widespread use of buck-eye couplings meant that the few breakdowns that did lead to accidents had, on the whole, decreasingly serious consequences. The events in this chapter, influenced in part by the after effects of the Second World War, represent a concentrated period of exceptions to the general rule that dangerous engine failures had become rare. There were at that time eighteen main loco

workshops employing a total of some 38,000 staff – a ratio of about two men to every engine in service. The average number of miles a locomotive travelled in 1952 for every defect that occurred – most, of course, trivial and not affecting services – was up to 30,000. This was twice as good a figure as that of a few years previously.

With the end of steam on British Rail – the oil-fired little locos in the Vale of Rheidol excepted of course – the improvement has been easier to sustain with the relatively simple diesels and electrics that now ply the remaining tracks. Coal-fired steam engines, regarded by many today as works of art, were not always thought of so lovingly by those whose long working hours were devoted to cleaning and servicing them. We owe those railwaymen quite a debt for the generally high standards they maintained.

101

13
Sutton Coldfield
(London Midland Region, BR)

Derailments whilst negotiating curves have always been a feature of railway operation, and excessive speed has nearly always been to blame. In the first decade of the century there were four major accidents of this kind: one at Aylesbury and the three at Salisbury, Grantham and Shrewsbury known collectively as 'The Midnight Runaways' (see *Trains to Nowhere*). Between them they accounted for sixty-four deaths. It was twenty-six years before there was another serious incident of this kind; that was on the old LMS Port Carlisle branch at Canal Junction in Carlisle when, in 1931, a train took the 10-chain bend there at three times the 15 mph limit and three passengers died as a result – a toll that only narrowly missed being very much higher. As usual the cause was driver error, but the Inspector, Lt-Col Mount, pointed out that the lack of lineside indications of prevailing speed restrictions had not assisted him and suggested keeping distant signals at danger on the approaches to such curves. The latter idea was not new but the Carlisle affair led to much more widespread adoption of the practice. This no doubt contributed to the fact that it was to be

another quarter of a century or so before the next significant accident occurred due to a train being driven too fast into a bend.

On Sunday 23 January 1955, at Sutton Coldfield in the West Midlands, there took place the last disastrous derailment of a steam train on a curve in Britain. Seventeen people were killed and, as with most of these runaways, no really satisfactory explanation was ever found for the driver's disregard of an established restriction on a line with which he was perfectly familiar. Like other of his predecessors in similar circumstances, he did not survive to throw any light on his lapse.

Sutton Coldfield is on the line from Lichfield (City) to Birmingham. In 1955, as now, it normally carried only a local train service and a few slow freight trains. It has, however, long provided a useful alternative route for expresses running between Yorkshire and the South West when the main line via Tamworth has been under repair. On the day in question such diversions were in force. It was a winter Sunday with no service booked to stop along the line and the station was therefore closed and the signal box switched out.

36. Sutton Coldfield. Recovery work in progress the next day. The remains of the leading coach have been cleared from the centre foreground, part of its 30-year-old all-timber bodywork can be seen on the platform behind the engine. All the other coaches were newer with steel-panelled bodies. The third one has been partially lifted off the wreck of the fourth, and the fifth carriage is rammed under the down platform awning and is the focus of attention of the men seen in that vicinity. Even the somewhat superior construction of these two vehicles could not prevent them sustaining substantial damage as the constrictions of the station compressed the wreckage as the train piled up.

The 12.15 pm midday York–Bristol express, comprising ten coaches, reached Derby at about 3.10 pm – thirty minutes late. The 63-year-old driver, Martin, and his fireman, Howell, both of Gloucester Motive Power Depot, took over from the Sheffield men in the cab of the Bristol-based class 5 mixed-traffic 4–6–0 engine, no. 45274. The oncoming crew were told that it was riding a bit roughly with some knocking in the axle boxes.

When a through driver was unfamiliar with the diversion route, an indigenous driver was provided as a conductor. It was, and is, a standard practice in these situations. Martin had been over the road before, during previous

103

engineering works on the main line, and he and Howell had brought a northbound train up that way earlier in the day; but he did not know it well enough to satisfy the rules, so a pilot driver was assigned for each of his runs. The man designated for the role on this return trip was known slightly to Martin. His name was Allen and, at fifty-four, he was fully experienced. He had been a driver for seventeen years and had been based in the area throughout his thirty-seven years on the railway, driving both passenger and freight trains through Sutton Coldfield innumerable times.

Driver Allen joined the train at Burton-on-Trent and Martin stood behind him as he took control of the locomotive. The rules decreed that a conductor-driver must actually drive the train he was escorting if he was qualified to handle the particular type of engine in use. There were no class 5s at the depot where he was based, but he had often had occasion to drive them when relieving at other sheds in the area where they were plentiful. In any case the layout of the controls was practically identical to that of the 2–6–4 tank engines that were used for the passenger services over the line, though these were somewhat less powerful machines. The opportunity to drive an express did not come his way all that often and it had been six months since the last time he had been called upon to conduct such a train. This no doubt compensated for the fact that it had been his Sunday off and he had only been given a couple of hours' notice of this extra duty.

By cutting the generous station times, the train was running only fifteen minutes late by this point, and by the time they reached Lichfield Trent Valley High Level station, Allen, who was known to like to work an engine 'smartly', had recovered another four. At Lichfield they took on water, and Martin, satisfied that his colleague was competent to be left in

charge, decided to have a rest from the footplate over the remainder of the journey to New Street. Using as an excuse an old leg injury, aggravated he said by the rough riding of the engine, he took a seat in an empty compartment in the leading coach.

So, as the train left Lichfield at 3.58, now only ten minutes late, the footplate carried only Driver Allen and Fireman Howell. Up through Lichfield City station they went, and then, after the Walsall line had branched off to the right, they were off along the undulating route through Shenstone and Blake Street to the highest point near Four Oaks. Then it was down the 2-mile 1 in 100 incline and round the 30-chain right-hand bend into the tunnel immediately preceding Sutton Coldfield station.

Since neither driver nor fireman survived the crash, we do not know how it was that the train entered this tunnel at over 55 mph instead of the 30 mph maximum speed allowed. It is clear from timings and lineside observations that it was running well over the 40 mph limit on the gradient before this point. All the passenger trains that Allen was used to driving over the line were booked to stop at Sutton Coldfield, however, and the freight trains he drove were not fast ones, so the observance of the restrictions here were normally automatic. But he had done conductor duty before and been in control of the engines; on no previous occasion had he failed to keep down to a safe speed.

The tunnel is just over 170 yards long and is straight, but a few yards beyond begins a left-hand curve with a nominal radius of 15 chains. At that time the curve sharpened at one point to about 8 chains before easing again to 15 through the station. This 'knuckle', introduced when installing a trailing crossover, was eliminated when realigning the track after the derailment. The express burst out of the tunnel and into this eccentric arc at around twice the permitted

Fox Photos

37. Sutton Coldfield. The sad state of the class 5 4–6–0 after it had demolished the platform edge and skidded onto the platform itself. The furthest point of its travel has been marked in chalk on the wall in the centre foreground to assist in the painstaking investigation of cause and effect that is already under way. An inverted section of the first coach is seen on the right. It was one of the first built by the newly formed LMS after the Grouping.

maximum speed and the enormous centrifugal force thus exerted threw it towards the opposite platform as the train entered the station. The engine, tender and first four coaches ran along against the edge of the down platform until the locomotive overturned and demolished it further on near the far end. The leading coach, with the horrified Martin aboard, was virtually destroyed, as were the fourth and fifth ones as the train piled up within the restricting confines of the station. Only the last carriage remained on the rails.

There were about 300 passengers on board the express. Twelve were killed outright, with two more and a railwayman dying later in hospital. Driver Martin, although in one of the worst affected vehicles, survived the disaster but was amongst the many seriously injured.

Another express going in the opposite direction was already in section and in grave danger of running into the wreckage. However, a ticket inspector, Attenborough, and an off-duty fireman, Smith, who were travelling in the crashed train, rushed to the empty signal box, just beyond the south end of the down platform, and put all the signals to danger. The down train was thereby brought safely to a stop at the home signal. Such commendable initiative by these two trainmen almost certainly averted an appalling double disaster. A couple of lineside residents who were in their garden just beyond the station also thought to try and stop any oncoming traffic but it seems unlikely that they could have given the train sufficient warning to avoid some degree of collision.

The Investigating Inspector, Lt-Col G. R. S. Wilson, could discover no defect in the wrecked train's engine or its brakes that could have accounted for the excessive speed or have contributed to the derailment. Driver Allen had, it seemed, simply forgotten the restrictions governing this stretch of line. It had so rarely, in his extensive experience of the route, been necessary to think about the limits imposed and, perhaps, the exhilaration of his unexpected task was sufficiently distracting. He was after all, probably for the first time, in charge of an express without supervision. Driver Martin should, of course, have been there. Whether or not his presence would have made a difference is a matter of conjecture, as there was nothing to inform him of the speed restrictions, and he might have been disinclined to interfere with the man specifically assigned to take the train over a road he knew intimately.

If he could not adequately explain Allen's extraordinary behaviour, the Inspector could at least draw attention to something that could be done to lessen the chance of another such event. Had Martin stayed on the footplate he might have taken some action, and indeed Allen might not have made his tragic mistake, if there had been lineside speed signs. Such signs had not up to then been a general feature of British railway practice for permanent restrictions. Only the LNER had been in the habit of marking such limits before nationalisation, and even then only the principal ones were covered. British Railways eventually extended the use of these white (now yellow) cut-out numbers throughout the country. Lt-Col Wilson's comments here doubtless accelerated the process considerably. Until then the observance of speed restrictions had been largely left to the knowledge of routes by drivers who were required to confirm their knowledge by signature on every turn of duty. Distant signals were also kept at danger on many high speed lines where a significant speed reduction was called for. Since there had been no major failure to comply on plain track since the Carlisle derailment, the practices would seem to have generally worked well; but because of the calamitous consequences that could result from just one lapse it was obviously not enough.

Even with speed signs there have been later examples of this kind of accident. In 1962 at Lincoln, in a peculiarly similar incident, a diesel-hauled Scottish express from King's Cross, being driven by another conductor-driver over a diversion, came off the rails while doing 55 mph round a sharp curve with a 15 mph limit clearly signed. In that case the local driver was not qualified to drive the class of locomotive concerned and very much underestimated his approach speed. Three died in that crash, with around fifty others injured. Another such Scotland-bound express from King's Cross came off a bend at Morpeth in 1969 when travelling at twice the permitted 40 mph. Six were killed there and well over 100 injured. The driver admitted that his mind had wandered and he had forgotten where he was and had not seen the speed sign.

The Morpeth accident led to ATC magnetic inductors, of the Automatic Warning System type developed by British Railways, being installed where substantial speed reduction was necessary on lines with a basic speed of 75 mph or more. Such an advance, highly desirable though it was, would not, of course, have prevented the Sutton Coldfield instance, nor others like the one at Eltham Well Hall in 1972, which have happened since on lines with lower limits. Col Robertson, who presided at both the Morpeth and Eltham inquiries, did not feel that the exceptional circumstances of the latter derailment (where alcohol was the principal factor) called for the qualifying speed for AWS installation to be reduced.

Now, with severe financial restraints on our railways apparently here to stay, it is unlikely that the money will be forthcoming for further extension of automatic warning in this field. It is still very much up to the man in the cab to be always alert and responsible. Travelling in the security of a train we are very much in his hands and he has rarely let us down.

14
Chapel-en-le-Frith
(London Midland Region, BR)

The story of Driver John Axon is another of those stirring classic tales of heroism that spring from the innate courage of many apparently ordinary men and women. It is a virtue seen often in the artificial ambience of war, when emotions are heightened by the unaccustomed proximity to persistent and extreme danger; but it is rare for the average man in his normal civilian employment to meet a situation that calls on any reserves of physical courage that he may have. Many a potential hero or heroine no doubt dies elderly in bed, untested. Others are tested and found wanting of this attribute; but it is a heartening fact that many people called upon to display bravery of an unselfish kind seem to rise to the occasion admirably.

The quaintly (not to say lengthily) named small market town of Chapel-en-le-Frith is in the Peak District of Derbyshire, about 5 miles north of Buxton. It used to have two stations: Central, on the old line to Derby, and South. The Central one was closed in 1967 and, with the now superfluous word 'South' removed, the other one became the town's only station. It is on the former LNWR line from Buxton to

Manchester and is in the middle of a 7-mile long incline from a summit between Buxton and Dove Holes down to Whaley Bridge. The gradient varies from 1 in 58 to 1 in 70, easing to 1 in 150 through Dove Holes and Chapel-en-le-Frith stations. Apart from being steep, it is also a continuously curving stretch of line north of Dove Holes.

On Saturday 9 February 1957, Driver Axon and his fireman, Scanlon, started their turn of duty at 5.30 am and their engine that day was a class 8F 2–8–0 tender engine, no. 48188. It was one of many engines to which they might have been assigned and they were no more familiar with it than with the many other essentially identical locomotives at Stockport Edgeley Shed. Their first job that Saturday was to take an up freight from Adswood to Buxton. The engine was steaming well and appeared to be in good order, although Axon did notice that the regulator was rather stiff. They set off and took their train of twenty-three wagons up the long climb from Whaley Bridge to Dove Holes and over the summit for the short 1 in 66 descent into Buxton. On this falling gradient the steam brake worked satisfactorily but there was a

Press Association

38. Chapel-en-le-Frith. No. 48188 where it ended its downhill dash amid the combined wreckage of both its own wagons and those of the train into which it crashed. Its tender lies twisted round behind it with its rear end in the air. The demolished signal box is behind the canopy on the left. The damaged diesel mutliple unit has been towed away from the foreground where it was hit by the locomotive. The pall of coal and lime dust has settled leaving an unpleasant coating on most of the scene. Firemen are still much in evidence – indicating the protracted danger of fire amongst so much combustible cargo.

small escape of steam coming from the union nut between the pipe and the driver's brake valve. It was a frequent occurrence to have a wisp of steam coming from these joints, for the nuts tended to loosen as a result of ordinary footplate vibration, but Axon sensibly decided to get the leak attended to before making the return trip.

A fitter came to look at it and stopped the leak by tightening the nut a quarter-turn, which was a common cure for a common fault and virtually any other fitter would have done the same. Unbeknown to him, however, another driver had watched another fitter make a similar adjustment to check the same symptom the previous day at Warrington. Had he known, or had the seeping steam not ceased when he turned the

39. Chapel-en-le-Frith. A view from behind the remains of the signal box on the up side – its name board lying undamaged amidst the shattered woodwork. The engine cab in which John Axon so bravely died is on the right of the picture under the wheels of the upturned tender.

spanner, he would have unscrewed the nut to investigate further and thus discovered that the brazed collar underneath had become distorted, by repeated overtightening of the nut, and a crack had developed. As it was, the fitter's extra quarter-turn, although it temporarily sealed the crack, exerted the final straw of pressure on the underlying collar and he walked away from the engine leaving behind him a virtual time bomb.

With the problem apparently solved, Axon and his mate set off back towards Stockport at 11.5 am with a train of thirty-three wagons, mostly of coal, which they were to take through to Warrington. It had developed into a dry, clear day. Running chimney-first, they were assisted up the 1¾ miles to the summit by an unattached banking engine which kept working hard against the brake van. Their speed up the incline had risen to about 15 mph when the wisp of steam started to hiss again. Axon and Scanlon bound a couple of rags round the joint and tied them tightly, but the leak got worse and soon was blowing out in a cloud.

Driver Axon told his fireman that he thought they might make it into the loop that started at Bibbington's Sidings, just over the summit, where they were due to stop to pin down wagon brakes for the descent. Once there they could get help. But just as they reached the Bibbington's distant signal there was a deafening bang and the cab was filled with scalding steam which drove both men back onto the tender. After recovering from the shock, they screwed down the tender's handbrake and then tried to reach the regulator. They made repeated attempts but the force and heat of the steam was too intense. At last, using a fire iron, Scanlon managed to knock it partly closed but, with the banking engine still pushing hard (its crew unaware that anything was amiss), the speed was not noticeably reduced. They were now just about to reach the summit, with the long steep slope beyond, and Axon told his mate to jump clear and try and drop as many wagon brakes as he could. His fireman obeyed and managed to drop six or seven handles but the train was moving too fast for him to pin them down so they had little effect. As the brake van came by, he shouted to the guard to apply his brake, but that didn't seem to help much either.

As the train pulled away from him, he ran to the banking engine which was slowing down having completed its task. The driver had seen the guard wrestling with his brake and noticed that the train had drawn away faster than was usual and so was half prepared for Scanlon's story of the broken steam pipe and the regulator still in second position. Scanlon climbed aboard and they went on to Bibbington's Sidings signal box to put the man on duty there, Bowyer, in the picture. They then went on as far as Dove Holes searching the line in the hope of finding Axon if he too had jumped off.

But he had not. Once over the top of the hill the train had turned onto the loop line and was gaining speed rapidly down the 1 in 70 gradient to Dove Holes where the loop ended. Axon was still struggling to get the regulator closed further but the steam was escaping even more fiercely making an impassable barrier. He must have cursed himself for not having had something done about the stiffness in the regulator that he had noticed first thing that morning. Scanlon's lucky hit with the fire iron might have been a crucial bit more effective if he had. But there was no time to ponder on might-have-beens with the train racing downhill to possible disaster. With his coat wrapped round his head to afford some protection, and ignoring the pain from the scalds which were by now extensive, he continued to try and regain control of his engine. The end of the loop was now only a little way ahead and it was imperative that he attract the attention of the signalman there, as it was apparent from the signals that he was expected to stop.

Dove Holes signal box lay just beyond the end of the loop, ahead of the down platform. Signalman Fox had seen a preceding down goods train off towards Stockport less than five minutes before getting the 'Train Entering Section' signal from Bibbington's Sidings box for Axon's train. He sent his acceptance and was then required to deal with a freight train going the other way which was just entering the up loop. This meant that he did not see the runaway until it was close to the home signal. He saw steam pouring out of the cab and Axon's frantic efforts to catch his glance. He had intended to hold the train there to allow a passenger train to overtake it and so the points were set for the trap siding. Correctly interpreting Axon's gesticulations, he had only a moment to weigh up the alternatives – for the engine had been only 80 yards from the loop exit points when he had first seen it and it was travelling now at some 25 mph.

He could let the train run straight on into the trap siding from which it would crash through his cabin and into the end of the station wall with serious results – not least to himself unless he got out fast; or he could set the points to take it back onto the main line and hope that the driver could stop it before it caught up with the train he had so recently sent on ahead. Fox could not know, of course, that the brakes were completely out, nor that the regulator could not be closed nor the reverse gear engaged. So, not knowing that the driver had no chance of stopping in the available distance on the main line, in view of the gradient, he decided to opt for possible salvation instead of definite disaster – and who could blame him for that?

He unlocked the loop points and reversed them in the nick of time just as the leading wheels were almost upon them. The train swung across, clattering over them with all the wagons successfully holding the rails. Instead of sending the 4–5–5 'Train Running Away On Right Line' signal to the next box, which was Chapel-en-le-Frith, he decided to telephone the signalman there to brief him quickly on the essential facts as he knew them.

Axon, relieved at the reprieve, was, of course, unaware that he was so close behind another train as this had left Buxton nearly twenty minutes before him. As far as he knew the next train ahead was the 10.54 am diesel passenger out of Buxton and that should have been well clear by this time. He did not know that Fox had held the earlier freight at Dove Holes and let the 10.54 pass it. He continued with his efforts to reach the regulator; whether or not he succeeded in finally reaching it isn't known, but it was found to be shut when the engine was examined

two hours later and no one else claimed to have closed it after the accident, so perhaps he did. The reversing gear was found to be still in the full forward position though. The closure of the regulator would have meant that, if the line had been clear, the train might well have come to a stop on the slight upward slope at Disley. On the other hand, since it could easily have touched 80 mph at the bottom of the long gradient it was presently descending, it might well have been derailed on one of the various sharp curves before that. As we know, however, the line was *not* clear so we must discard the 'ifs' of conjecture.

Signalman Howe, who was on duty in Chapel-en-le-Frith box, had a two-coach up diesel passenger train from Manchester waiting to go on to Buxton. The train ahead of it was the goods that had been going into the up loop at Dove Holes and Howe was waiting for the signal from Fox to enable him to clear the passenger train forward. Since they had been held by the starting signal for over a minute after the scheduled departure time, the guard of the DMU went into the box, which was at the end of the up platform, to comply with Rule 55. He had only been in the box for a few seconds when the call came from Fox to tell of the approaching runaway.

The down freight train in front of Axon's had been moving fairly slowly and was only just now approaching them. It was doing 20 mph as it came towards the station and Howe could not predict where the likely collision would occur, so he told the DMU's guard to warn his passengers and get them out of the way. The guard rushed off and he and the platform staff hurried the passengers off the train and out into the station forecourt. They also signalled to the driver of the freight train, indicating that he should accelerate. The DMU's driver stabbed his finger in the direction of the overtaking

40. Chapel-en-le-Frith. The wreckage seen from the down side. The petrol wagon was luckily empty. With 150 tons of loose coal lying around and a roaring fire in the loco it could have proved an horrendous conflagration. The fire brigade was quickly there to ensure that did not happen.

disaster, hoping that the crew might look back and see Axon's locomotive catching them up.

Unfortunately the most vulnerable member of the crew, the guard, was too far back to be alerted by all this activity and he received no warning that might have enabled him to escape from his most perilous position.

The engine of this train, which was of the same type as Axon's and also running chimney-first, was in the hands of Driver Butler and Fireman Bradshaw. They had approached the station blissfully unaware that anything was wrong. As they passed through the station, Bradshaw had noticed a number of people shouting and waving their arms about. He could not hear what they were calling and could not make out why some seemed to be waving them on and others pointing back up the line. He glanced back but could see nothing unusual and was generally mystified. Realising that his

113

driver, being on the down platform side, had probably not seen any of this exhibition, he told him that he thought there was 'something going on' and this time they both looked back. Butler saw a wagon oscillating and then a 'belch of smoke'; this was followed by the impact of the collision which sent a shock wave through the train derailing four wagons near the front. Their engine was driven forward nearly 300 yards by the force before Butler could stop it. He and Bradshaw were shaken but unhurt.

Even with slightly more warning it is unlikely that Butler could have done much more than 'gather' the train as most of the wagons were pinned down for the long descent. It might, however, have moved the point of collision to a site beyond the station and avoided thereby the devastation it suffered. But once again we are in the realms of hypothesis.

Axon's engine had burst out of Eaves tunnel, 3/4 mile away, in a cloud of steam and smoke like a demented dragon on the rampage. With its tail of rattling trucks, it had raced down the 1 in 58 slope at around 55 mph watched with horror by the railwaymen at the station. The guard's van of the other train, with its unsuspecting occupant, was just passing the down home signal – 70 yards before the platforms – when the 2–8–0 smashed into the back of it. The van and the rear three wagons were completely shattered and the guard was killed. Axon was thrown to the floor as his engine ploughed on and its tender demolished the signal box hurling Howe onto the sidings below. Mercifully, and miraculously, he was more shaken than hurt by the experience – one that his colleague at Dove Holes had had the opportunity of avoiding, little knowing that he was passing it on down the line to Howe. The equipment in the box was destroyed and the block and telephone connections severed. The signals were all pulled to the clear position by tightened wires.

In the last throes of this devastating discharge of energy, no. 48188 struck the front of the DMU and came to rest lying on its side against the up platform wall. The leading thirty wagons were piled up on top of the rear vehicles of the train in front and formed a heap of debris 25 feet high which blocked both the lines for nearly three days. The guard of the runaway train, who had stayed at his post to the end, with the ineffectual brake held on with a brake stick, found that his van and the wagon next to it were the only vehicles of his train still on the rails.

The track was badly damaged for more than 1/4 mile and a pall of coal and lime dust hung over the havoc for quite some time. Steps were quickly taken to summon the emergency services and to protect the line in both directions with detonators. The telephone in the station-master's office was still working so the boxes on either side were easily warned by way of that. The wires had to be cut, though, to get the signals back down to 'danger'.

Driver John Axon was dead when they got to him. His heroic conduct, when like Brewer and Rawlings at Braysdown, he could easily have jumped to his own safety, was to earn him the George Cross and an honoured place in the history, not only of railways, but of humanity. This may have been little compensation for him, but was some consolation for the loved ones he left behind.

In his inquiry into the accident, Brigadier C. A. Langley added his voice to the paean of praise and concluded that the accident was one of those unfortunate events that only in a perfect world would have been foreseen. It was to be regretted that the distorted collar in the steam brake joint had not been detected, but it was not unreasonable that it had not been. All these joints were replaced after the accident with ones of a safer design. Bowyer, the signalman at Bibbington's Sidings, who had been there nearly a year and was familiar with the normal pattern of movements, might have thought more of the train's behaviour: its speed was unusually high and it did not stop to pin down wagon brakes before going into the loop. Yet neither factor was unprecedented in itself and the latter was almost usual; the pinning down often being done on the loop. He had noticed a lot of steam coming from the engine but did not associate it with trouble on the footplate and did not think it anything much out of the ordinary. That he was alert was demonstrated by the fact that he had noticed that the tail lamp, for some unrecorded reason, was missing on the brake van and he had sent the appropriate signal ahead. Had he decided that the other signs merited sending a 'Train Running Away . . .' signal, just in case, it might have been passed on to Howe in time for him to give more effective warning to Butler and by that means move the site of the crash further down the line. More particularly it might have meant that the guard of Butler's train could have been told and he could have jumped out. On balance though, the Inspector thought that it would probably not have materially affected events as they transpired.

Everyone else had acted properly, Scanlon also bravely in battling against the scalding steam, and there was much to commend. The only thing that could have averted the disaster once the pipe had come adrift would have been automatic vacuum braking throughout the train. This would have stopped the train in comfortable time despite the gradient. Conversion to this system on freight trains was already well under way, with 200,000 due to be thus equipped before the end of 1958, and the plan was to cover all rolling stock as soon as practicable.

Some heroes go unsung; not so John Axon.

An acclaimed radio documentary called, and featuring, 'The Ballad Of John Axon' brought his story in novel form to a wide audience. It was a song of praise well worth the singing. Like Ben Gimbert and Jim Nightall of Soham fame, he too has been further immortalised by having a locomotive belatedly named after him. A class 86 electric locomotive, no. 86261, was christened 'Driver John Axon GC', and keeps his memory running along the metals. No scalding vapour could ever challenge the driver of such a machine. The jobs of footplatemen in Britain have undergone a transformation so major that it seems highly unlikely that a driver will ever again have so tragically tested the tensile strength of his mettle.

John Axon's story brings us to the end of this second selection of accidents involving steam trains on Britain's railways this century. The iron roads and their steam horses, that revolutionised travel throughout the world, began in this country. They represent man's ingenuity and industry at its most productive. The railways have ever been ready to learn from their mistakes, though not always as expeditiously as they might, and from primitive beginnings their safe operation has developed by trial, error and disaster to a level that compares very favourably with that of other forms of transport. It is a demonstrable fact that a seat in a train is a pretty safe place to be – especially if it's a British train.

A study of accidents is a study of much of the nature of Man and, in seeking to see how and why these trains have come to grief, I have found the human element quite as compelling as the intrinsic railway one. It was this factor that made the subject of such particular interest to J. A. B. Hamilton as well. I hope it is an interest that we have been able to share with you.

Index